C000257901

from **ADVERSITY** *to*
FREEDOM

from ADVERSITY to
FREEDOM

· · · · · · · · · ·

MICHAEL
CUNNINGHAM

Bridge-Logos

Alachua, Florida 32615

Bridge-Logos

Alachua, FL 32615 USA

From Adversity to Freedom

by Michael Cunningham

Copyright ©2013 by Bridge-Logos, Inc.

All rights reserved. Under International Copyright Law, no part of this publication may be reproduced, stored, or transmitted in any form or by any means—printed, written, electronic, mechanical, photographic (photocopy), recorded, or otherwise—except for brief quotations, without written permission from the Publisher.

Printed in the United States of America.

Library of Congress Catalog Card Number: 2013954416
International Standard Book Number 978-1-61036-113-2

All Scripture quotations, references and Bible notes in this book are from The Spirit-Filled Life® Bible, The New King James Version. Copyright ©1991 by Thomas Nelson, Inc.

CH 12-04-13

Dedication

I DEDICATE this book to my late wife, Geraldine, who walked this road with me and who was also my best friend. In addition, her walk with the Lord and her faith and trust in Jesus were an inspiration to me. I will be forever grateful to the Lord for joining us as man and wife. The Lord blessed her with much strength.

Also, to my five wonderful children: Marc, Matthew, Simon, Elena, and Jessica whom God used to refine me and who have been absolute blessings to me. I am so proud of them all.

Most importantly, my sincere gratitude to our heavenly Father for His display of unconditional love towards us. To our Lord Jesus for His truth and grace, and to the Holy Spirit for His faithful help to me in recalling all the important details which I needed to complete this book, and for enabling me to give a testimony after all these years of walking with Him.

Contents

Foreword

MICHAEL CUNNINGHAM is a man of God. He loves the Lord with all his heart, mind, soul, and strength, and He wants others to love God as well. That's one of the reasons why he has written this very moving and uplifting book, which is far more than an autobiography.

In *From Adversity to Freedom,* Michael Cunningham shows us how to depart from the world of darkness and enter into God's marvelous kingdom of light in spite of any obstacles we may encounter along the way. His writing is poignantly open and honest, and after reading his outstanding book, you will want to take a spiritual pilgrimage like Michael's.

This is a very encouraging book that shows us how to apply the Word of God to our lives so that we will experience God's grace, love, and blessing. Do you want to be an overcomer? Do you want to be more than a conqueror? Do you want to live above the circumstances of your life?

If your answer to these questions is yes, you will want to read this book—a book that reveals how exciting it is to live the adventurous life of faith. Michael reveals how to overcome all hurts, fear, and discouragement. When his beloved wife, Geraldine, died, He experienced God's grace in a fuller measure than ever before, and he wants so much for you to experience, as he did, all God has for you.

There are unlimited possibilities awaiting you! This book will help you to know what some of those possibilities are. As a disciple of Jesus who wants to learn and grow, you can enter into an obedient relationship with the Lord that will bring success, prosperity, health, and victory to you. You can know God in all His faithfulness and love.

Michael shares stories from his own life that you will be able to relate to. You will enjoy reading about his boyhood, his conversion experience, his courtship and marriage, the births of his five children, various miraculous healings, and so many other important events in his life. You will walk alongside him as he develops a close relationship with the Lord.

Through personal illustrations and biblical teaching, Michael leads us into our own deep, personal relationship with the Lord Jesus Christ. He helps us to understand what it means to be an obedient disciple. He provides us with biblical teachings that will buttress our faith.

Thank you so much, Michael, for being a transparent disciple of the Lord who wants us all to see what you've seen, to know what you know, and to experience what you've experienced. I pray that as you read this book, you will be changed and drawn closer to our heavenly Father. You are a blessing to the Body of Christ and indeed to all those who are on that quest for hope, peace and security.

May God bless you as you continue your exciting walk with the Lord.

I am pleased to be the publisher of your very moving and inspiring book. May it find its way into the hands and hearts of thousands of people around the world.

It is indeed a God-glorifying book, and it reflects the touch and encouragement of the Holy Spirit on you as you compiled it.

Lloyd Hildebrand
Publisher
Bridge-Logos, Inc.

Introduction

FOR nearly all of my Christian life, God has given me a deep desire to see His kingdom come and His will be done here on Earth. As well, He has given me the vision to be able to see His power manifested here in our midst. I also wanted to be able to see the stronghold that the enemy has had over our lives broken and in turn see Christ formed in us. The Lord has given me gifts of encouragement and faith and my hope is that as you read my story the Lord will ignite a similar fire in your belly for the things of God.

I believe my story demonstrates that by applying the Word of God to everyday living we can and will live a successful, prosperous and secure life. We will have struggles, of course, but if we continue to submit to God, we will overcome and conquer in the end.

Another personal desire is to demonstrate that the Word of God is trustworthy. The Lord, by His Word and His Holy Spirit, challenges our sinful nature, and He will never cross the boundary of our free will. However, if we yield to Him, embrace Him and live by His Word, we enter a strong fortress of protection. To people who have suffered in their life experience, I say *"Indeed, let God be true..."* (Romans 3:4). *"Seek after God with all your heart and He will be found by you" (Jeremiah 29:13).*

I, with my late wife, Geraldine, have shown how we have translated and applied the Word of God to many aspects of our lives and we have seen that the secret to success is obedience to God's instruction.

The Gospel of John 14:21 instructs us that, *"He who has My commandments and keeps them, it is he who loves me. And he who loves Me will be loved by My Father, and I will love him and manifest Myself to him."*

I have personally experienced the truth of this Scripture. The Scripture shows us that the way we show our love to the Father is by obeying His Word. When we do this, we receive further revelation of the Lord Jesus Christ by way of further insight, understanding, wisdom, discernment and direction. All of these truths lead to success in life and, more importantly, to eternal life.

Since my wife died four years ago, I have been especially diligent in obeying the Lord's instructions. As a result, He has opened my mind and has directed me into wonderful *new things,* with unlimited possibilities. Where my thinking was *small,* He has extended my horizons. God makes a way where there seems to be no way. Therefore, we must keep pressing onwards towards the goal.

I hope to share with you, the reader, how great God is. In our normal world of little faith, our conception of God is not the miracle-working mighty God of the Acts of the Apostles. People who come to trust and experience God for themselves will begin to prove what Scripture says: ***"Now to Him who is able to do exceedingly abundantly above all that we ask or think, according to the power that works in us, to Him be glory in the church by Christ Jesus to all generations, forever and ever. Amen" (Ephesians 3:20-21).***

Come and let Jesus do great and mighty things in your life as He has done in mine.

I hope this book demonstrates that being a disciple of Jesus is a process; it shows that it is about a daily relationship. The many stories you will read show that there are difficulties in this daily relationship. Being a disciple is not always easy, but it is always worthwhile. Discipleship, which involves obedience to Him, changes us into the image of Christ more and more each day as we obey Him. In my own case, I am not the same man that I was when I started out as a disciple thirty years ago. The appendix at the end of the book explains the journey to discipleship.

Chapter 1

The Swim Race

W HEN I was a young boy—about twelve years old or thereabouts—I started swimming seriously! My mother taught me how to swim and, when I had built up a bit of speed and had become quite competent in the water, she approached the local Galway swimming club coach, Jimmy Cranny, and persuaded him to let me enter a 50-metre race on the day of the next swimming gala. He was reluctant to enter me in the race and thereby took no responsibility for me, as he had never seen me swim. Eventually, he said yes to my mother, but he added that if I got into difficulties during the race that she would have to go into the water and rescue me herself. She agreed, but knew she would not have to do any rescuing.

The swimming gala was a yearly fixture held on the shore of Galway Bay on a Sunday afternoon sometime during the summer and the location was on the west side of the Blackrock diving tower at the end of the promenade. The only thing that defined the 50-metre line away from the diving tower was a big timber boom floating on the top of the water, fixed securely to a vertical pole that was stuck into a permanent concrete structure to mark the 50-metre distance away from the concrete structure of the diving tower. The other end of the boom was tied to the rocks on the shoreline parallel to the tower. It was rough and ready in those days surely.

I am talking about the early 1960s. The summers, as I recall, were for the most part warm and sunny. Whenever there was an event like an outdoor swimming gala, half the town's population turned up to see and support it. There were very few distractions in those days, not like today. Even though the day was warm and sunny, it was rarely ever calm and windless.

This particular Sunday it was windy which meant that during the swim we had to contend with waves that could reach 12 to

1

24 inches, or 300mm to 600mm in height. This meant that when we took a breath of air during our swim a wave of water could overwhelm our windpipes and we would have to try to cough that out and still swim as hard as we could.

Whenever there was a 50-metre swim at this location, the race started at the timber boom so we would finish at the concrete diving tower where the judges could observe correctly those who came in order of placing. It also meant that when we started the race we were already in the water without any platform to spring from, left to our own abilities to propel ourselves forward with our arms and legs flapping like ducks to get the momentum going.

There was always a tremendous buzz of excitement at these events. Extended families and friends all gathered to cheer on every participant. Everybody knew everybody else and there was a great sense of community and of course rivalry. The adrenaline pumped! Since I was the new boy on the block in my first race, nobody knew what to expect. I saw people watching me with suspicion hoping I would not beat their son in the race. Some things never change!

I can't remember if anybody drove the message home to me about the importance of actually touching the finishing line to be considered for a place in the event.

My moment came, my first competitive swimming race ever, and my heart was thumping. I was very nervous. We had to make our way out to the timber boom—the start point. When all the swimmers for the race were calm in the water, we waited for the whistle to blow, "Go."

Well, it blew and we all began to propel ourselves frantically in the water to get moving. I charged down the 50 metres as fast as I could go and when I came within one metre of the finishing line—I stopped suddenly! I started to float in the water having a look around! I didn't realize that I had to touch the wall, which would indicate that I had completed the race. I saw all the other competitors come in after me. I suddenly heard spectators following the race, roaring and shouting at me trying to tell me, "Touch the wall! Touch the wall!" I had no idea why they were shouting at me; I just did not have a clue. I eventually touched the finishing line just to get out of the water.

Instead of hearing from the spectators "Well done, Michael, you did great!" all I heard was "Why didn't you touch the wall when you should have? You would have won the race."

As I said earlier, I cannot remember anybody really stressing upon me the necessity of touching the finishing line as fast as you can. As well as that, I had no idea of the prize awaiting me when I came in the first three, the silver cup or medal, the expression of well done. I tell you I soon learned and after that first race, I never failed to touch that finishing line as fast as I could, and even more importantly—to touch it first.

That day Jimmy Cranny saw me beat all his swimmers and saw the potential in me. He never let me out of his sight from then on. For the next seven to eight years after this event, I became the local and provincial swimming champion in most strokes and most distances. I was the person to beat. During those years, we had an annual prom swim, which continues today. It started at Blackrock diving tower and finished at Seapoint amusement centre, a distance of between 1,300 to 1,500 metres. During my years of swimming, I heard that people placed money bets on who was going to win. It gave me a most wonderful teenage life and those memories have and will stay with me for the rest of my life.

From that first race I made sure that I never entered a race without first of all making sure I was fit enough to finish it. If I were to swim a long distance I had to have a strategy of how I was to start it, how I would perform during it, making sure I had enough power to finish it well and fast if I needed to do it.

I absolutely loved swimming; I was so at ease in the water—just like a fish. I was so comfortable in it, and it was total pleasure for me. Then the competitive bug became very strong. The challenge and the thrill of the applause, the well done, the prize, the recognition, the sense of self-worth and the sense of achievement were electric and intoxicating. All these were in the mix.

To achieve all that, I had to train very hard and diligently. I could never expect to win all those races and be sitting at home doing nothing all week. I had to get up early every morning, cycle from my home to the canal beside the university for 8 a.m., and dive into the water that was so cold that it nearly gave me a heart attack. Discipline and focus were part of my life—I was serious about my swimming so I had to discipline my body and lifestyle if I was to succeed, and I did all that. I hasten to add that the training regime was not as vigorous as what children are expected to undergo these days, but it was still not a pushover. Little did I know that I was learning some spiritual principles completely unawares, or of how they would eventually change my life for the better.

Chapter 2

My Life Prior to and Just After Coming to Christ

I WAS born and reared in Galway, Ireland. I had a wonderful father and mother. I have three brothers and one sister.

My religious upbringing was in the Roman Catholic tradition and I was educated in the Jesuits College, Galway.

For me, school was not a good period in my life; I found it extremely difficult to concentrate on my subjects. I was always talking when I should not have been. I was a distraction and easily distracted. As a result, I always came last in the class but there was one particular week when a miracle happened! Back in those days, we had two-seater desks, and as an incentive to do well in school, they had a weekly medal for the boy who performed the best in his homework for that week. For one whole week, the boy who sat beside me was sick and absent from school. You will find it hard to believe the next bit. When the prefect of studies came around at the end of that particular week to give us our class placements, he was sure something had gone horribly wrong. I know now that he had no preview of the marks. Well, the poor man, he checked and re-checked my marks. But he had to succumb in the end and give me my marks. He gave me my place and I actually got first in the class that week—my one and only time!

Moving on from there, instead of concentrating on my school subjects I was always dreaming about sports, either organising events or playing on the teams.

I was a champion provincial swimmer. I won a Connacht schoolboy cap for rugby and was a good all-rounder. In my later teens, I began to play guitar and sing, including singing and acting in musicals, some cabaret and pub gigs. Life was full and wonderful.

After my second attempt, I finally passed my leaving cert (final secondary school exam) in 1972.

In 1970, when I was 18, my father died. I had only begun to talk to him and get to know him and suddenly he was gone. From then on, my heart searched for a father figure in an older man. It was a real void in my life. A mother's love is wonderful but a father's love, approval, and affirmation are vital ingredients, and I did not have them because he had died. My father's death left me very insecure.

In 1974, I entered the local technical college 3rd level education for a two-year course, but I did not finish it. In 1976, I went off to England where I worked as a builder's labourer and spent some time training to be a police officer. In 1977, I married a woman with whom I had swum competitively and later in that year, my first son, Marc, was born. Within a couple of weeks after Marc was born, I left the police force and returned home to Ireland. I took on various jobs, but due to accidents or being fed up, my jobs ended. My attitude to my wife was very negative. In my early years, I had many girlfriends and had observed too much dishonesty, deceit, unfaithfulness amongst couples both married and unmarried. With all that "background," my mind was not in good shape. I was damaged and mistrusting of people. I was unable to trust my wife and with a variety of jobs crumbling around me, my life was beginning to crumble. I wanted my own way; I was quick-tempered, stubborn and was unable to say sorry. I did not care whom I hurt. The future looked very bleak. My wife and I were renting a flat at my home, and, in March 1979, my marriage ended. There were too many negatives to handle. She just took our son with her and left.

In Autumn 1979, I went back to study the construction certificate course that I had failed to finish in 1976 and adding to that pressure I was pestered by lots of people enquiring about what went wrong with my marriage. Marriage breakup was a big thing in those days.

In May 1981, I finished the construction certificate course and got a job as an architectural draughtsman with a local company.

In October 1981, my wife divorced me in England and got

custody of our son. I deteriorated physically for a time and was on the verge of a nervous breakdown.

To return to spiritual matters—all these years I did not go to mass, confession, or Holy Communion, as I thought it was a waste of time. Every time I went to confession, I found myself repeating the same old sins saying to myself that this is useless. There is no power if nothing is changing. How strange it is, that in those days, even when everything was going against me, Jesus never entered my mind!

I wanted to be the master of me, calling all the shots, to be lord of my own life. I did not know that the Lord was at work. He had His eye on me.

During Christmas 1979, a priest named Father Bob McGoran, who had been the prefect of studies when I was at school, called to our house. He had been the man who had checked and re-checked my weekly marks for the weekly medal that I won on one occasion. He returned to Galway after being away for years and was working as parish priest in the Jesuit church. During this particular visit, he heard me sing and play guitar and asked if I would come to play and sing at the folk mass in his church. The objective of that particular mass was to attract young people. I agreed and found myself back in the Catholic Church after being absent for years.

Lo and behold a young man named Peter, the leader of the music group, was a born-again Christian. After some time, he felt at liberty to tell me that Jesus was Lord of his life and shared with me the love that God had for me. In addition, he told me that I could have a personal relationship with Jesus. He told me that he had invited Jesus into his life, and that he lived to do the will of Jesus first and foremost no longer living for his own will to be done. He told me that God loved us so much that He sent His only Son, Jesus, down to Earth to live and die on the Cross in order to pay the price for our sins. He told me about the unconditional love that God had for me and that Jesus wanted to bless me and give me eternal life. I only needed to put my trust in Him and come to believe and have faith in Him. In order for that to happen, I had to realise that I was a sinner in the first place and see my need for a Saviour. In reality, I was realising that I was not in right standing before God the Father as long as Jesus was not Lord of my life, and in my heart, I knew that I was a sinner. I can tell you honestly I was not used to this aspect of pure godly love.

The course of action that lay ahead of me was to repent of my sins. That is, to turn away from sinful living (disobeying His instructions), and start living to obey and thus please the Lord. I thought that this might prove too much for me. Deception was having its way in me. I found myself making excuses not to turn to the Lord. I told myself that I was all right and good enough and did not have any need to repent of my sins. I had small sins but they did not really matter. God would forgive me surely.

I saw that Peter was a good and happy man, and we became good friends. I often told him that I was all right the way I was and that he and his wife, Marian, could keep on praying for me. Little did I know at the time—they not only prayed diligently for me but also prayed that the veil that was over my eyes, blocking my vision of God, be removed so that I could see the glory of God the Father through Jesus.

Peter would occasionally tell me what the Lord did for him in his life. I was a patient listener. There were times when I would have said things or done some things that would have offended the Lord. Peter would then show me passages from the Bible indicating to me the Lord's thinking about what I did or said. I know now that on these occasions, the Holy Spirit was letting me know in a powerful way the state of my heart towards Him. Alongside that, my false sense of peace was being eroded, thus giving me a chance to come to my senses, but I was stubborn. Peter and Marian knew that God had His eye on me, and this encouraged them not to give up on me.

Peter and Marian were Spirit-filled Christians. Their relationship with the Lord had something of which I had no knowledge or understanding. That is, the love, the joy and peace that they had received from the Lord upon inviting Him into their hearts. They were compelled to talk about Him and had a real desire in their hearts to see everyone around them receive Jesus into their hearts. They knew what a change He would make in people's lives.

Every Sunday after the folk mass, Peter and I would go and play snooker and talk about the Lord, or, I should say that Peter would talk and I would listen. I had a foul mouth in those days, I also had a lot of anger stored up and every time I miscued the snooker ball, I would let out a curse word. You will see my reason for saying this later on.

Before I heard the gospel spoken about in this way, I felt I was all right and that someday I would get to Heaven, but I had no assurance of that. It was a hope without foundation. The Apostle John writes in Scripture, *"I have written these things so you may know that you have eternal life" (1 John 5:13).*

I wondered about eternity and life or death without end and I could not comprehend it, yet I never pursued it to find out more. All along, Peter was sharing with me, the Word of God, the consequences of sin, the God of all flesh and His love for each one of us. The concept of having a relationship with the Father through Jesus by the Holy Spirit who created Heaven, Earth, and every person who ever lived was mind blowing. I began to start thinking. Before this, I thought God was unreachable; therefore, why should I bother to waste my energy? However, the gospel that Peter introduced to me showed me that God was intensely interested in me and wanted to save me. That was a concept I never heard before.

All these truths ruffled my feathers and I was disturbed. I had not yet responded, but I was thinking now.

In the midst of all this hearing about the gospel from Peter, Marian, and their friends, I became suddenly aware and fear filled my heart. This fear said that if I gave my heart to the Lord, to let Him rule over me, He would take away from me all those things I treasured and held dear. I believed He was nothing but a killjoy. Those thoughts held me back for a very long time. Fear was rendering me inactive. Something else held me back also, my girlfriend. I did not want to give her up. I also knew in my heart that the relationship was not right before a holy God, but I did not want to come off *my* throne. As long as I was with her, there was no yielding to the Lord. The relationship eventually broke up, leaving the way clear to embrace the Lord.

During this time, I was in college studying. I had the added anxiety of a marriage breakup, study pressure, no income, insecurity, and being alone with very few friends. My family did not really understand what I was going through. Life was simply beginning to get on top of me. Eventually, having failed my second year exams in 1980, I reminded myself yet again of another failure! However, I took a deep breath, repeated it, and passed it in 1981.

In August 1981, things started looking up. I got a job as an architectural draughtsman in a local company, but was frustrated there and did not do well in the architectural division.

In April 1982, my boss came to me and said, "I wish you were not here but I won't sack you." That was all I needed to hear. It was getting unbearable for me there. I could not take any more. I made up my mind to try to immigrate to Australia. I could not get far enough away from home. I wanted to leave the place that filled me with so many disappointments and failures.

In May 1982, following the news about my boss telling me how he felt about me working for him, I took my two weeks annual leave plus two weeks without pay and went to Australia for a month. I wanted to see whether I would like it there and try to find an employer to sponsor me to immigrate there. I wanted to forget about that place.

While there, I was unable to find an employer to sponsor me but that did not deter me. I returned home and did all I could, and as quickly as possible, to get my immigration visa completed. It did not help when I was told that it could take up to two years for the embassy to reply to me. This news really frustrated me. I was screaming inside to get away from all that reminded me of failure.

My friends Peter and Marian continued to tell me that when someone hands over their lives to Christ, He would change their lives for the better. The truth of that statement comes from ***Jeremiah 29:11, which says, "For I know the thoughts that I think toward*** *you, says the Lord, thoughts of peace and not of evil, to give you a future and a hope."* However, I was not yet embracing it.

I was very afraid at this stage that if I invited Jesus into my life, He might stop me from going to Australia. I remember every Sunday at mass the priest would tell us to pray for our own intentions. Without fail I would ask the Lord that if Australia was for me, to either open or close the door to me. I would say to the Lord, that if He got me to Australia I would give Him my heart then. I thought that was a good bargain.

December 1982 came and I had a successful interview with the Australian Embassy. They told to me that if at the completion stage of my application the unemployment in Australia deteriorated they would have to refuse me entry. It was nerve-racking, as I did not know when that word would come back from the embassy. I lived in anxious hope.

On January 13, 1983, at 1 a.m., I could not take any more of the troubles and burdens in my life on my own. I cried out to Jesus sincerely to take over the direction of my life and become the Lord and Saviour of my life.

I repented to Him and made the decision to turn away from a self-centred sinful life and to live for Him and serve Him from that moment on. Peter had given me a guiding prayer to receive the Lord in advance of the time when I would say this prayer. Now that is faith! I read and said this prayer twice in case that God did not hear me. How daft can one get! Sure, it was He who drew me to himself in the first place. Scripture says, *"We love Him because He first loved us" (1 John 4:19).* In another verse, Jesus says, *"... No one can come to Me unless it has been granted to him by My Father" (John 6:65).*

The first thing I did after I got out of bed that morning was to ring my friend Peter. I told him that I had given my heart to Jesus before I went to sleep the previous night. Did he rejoice in hearing the news! The next person I told the good news to was my mother. That confession to Peter sealed my salvation, for the Word of God says in the *Epistle to the Romans 10:9-13, "That if you confess with your mouth the Lord Jesus and believe in your heart that God has raised Him from the dead, you shall be saved. For with the heart one believes unto righteousness, and with the mouth confession is made unto salvation. For the scripture says, "whoever believes on Him will not be put to shame." For there is no distinction between Jew and Greek, for the same Lord over all is rich to all who call upon Him. For "whoever calls on the name of the Lord shall be saved."*

Two days later on January 15, 1983, I received a letter from the Australian embassy. They had written and posted it on the 13th of January (the morning I handed my life over to Jesus), refusing me entry to Australia because of the worsening unemployment situation. I could hardly believe the timing of all this. I could not wait to get away from here and yet, when I got this news I was able to say, "All right Lord, I am in your hands now."

I said to Jesus, "You have closed the door to Australia to me. My boss does not want me here and at this stage, I do not want to be here either. I need you to get me another job or else improve my situation here in this job."

One week later, a man in the structural side of the company decided to leave and go downtown to another job. The boss came to me saying, "Martin is leaving next week. I'm willing to put you in his position, I believe you will do well and I'll give you an increase in pay." If that was not the Lord's doing, I was at a loss as to whose doing it was! He said that if Martin had not left he was afraid he was going to have to talk to me more seriously. I thanked the Lord for His provision.

In His providence, the Lord shut the door to Australia but kept me in that company. He gave the boss the courage to keep me on and I performed 100 percent better in my new position. I began to experience the peace of Jesus in my life, a peace that the world could not give nor understand. Jesus was beginning to make me feel secure. I was beginning to see His mighty hand at work.

Now that I had come to the Lord, my friend Peter knew that it was very important for me to be taught the Word of God if I was to grow up and mature in Him. *Hosea 4:6* states: *"My people are destroyed for lack of knowledge,"* so in February of 1983, he introduced me to the Galway Christian Fellowship whose pastor was Graeme Wylie.

This was surely a new experience for me, to hear the Word of God preached by my new pastor. In *John 6:63, Jesus says, "It is the Spirit who gives life; the flesh profits nothing. The words that I speak to you are spirit, and they are life."*

The preaching and teaching of the Word of God really imparted life and nourishment to my soul. I began to realise that up to this point I was seriously malnourished spiritually. When Graeme taught from the Scriptures, it felt so personal to me and I thought that Graeme had revelation as to the condition of my heart, but he did not.

Hebrews 4:12-13 will throw a bit of light on this matter:

Verse 12: "For the word of God is living and powerful, and sharper than any two-edged sword, piercing even to the division of soul and spirit, and of joints and marrow, and is a discerner of the thoughts and intents of the heart.

Verse 13: And there is no creature hidden from His sight, but all things are naked and open to the eyes of Him to whom we must give account."

The cleansing process of my soul had begun. The hearing of the word and the presence of the Holy Spirit brought both light and conviction to my heart when it was necessary.

I certainly entered into a new life. I began to realise that the creator of Heaven and Earth loved me unconditionally, revealing His Father-care over me.

Another thing I began to notice was that the people and places around Galway that reminded me of all my failures did not bother me anymore. I was able to hold my head up high. I had found a new friend in Jesus, and on top of that, brothers and sisters in Christ with the same Spirit dwelling in each of them.

I noticed after some time that I could have a relationship

with a woman without it turning to sex. I was beginning to give out a love that was pure because I had received a love that was pure and holy from the Lord.

Going back to the week after I gave my heart to the Lord, I had my usual game of snooker with my friend Peter. I had many foul balls this night as well, but there was a difference this night that I was unaware of and Peter was not pointing out during the game. He asked me at the end of the night's snooker games, "Did you notice anything tonight?"

I said "No!"

He replied, "Over the last few years, whenever you had a foul ball in the snooker game, you had a foul mouth following it. This night, you had many foul balls during the games but you had **no** foul mouth."

I tell you, I did not have to work at getting rid of my bad language. Jesus took that one away. The slavery to it was over. Two months after that, I noticed that the redness and itch that I had on my chest, which developed after my marriage breakup and years of turmoil, had gone and it never returned.

I had entered into a life of faith and trust in the Lord Jesus. I have a few directives in the following verses:

Proverbs 3:5-6: *"Trust in the Lord with all your heart, and lean not on your own understanding; in all your ways acknowledge Him, and He shall direct your paths."*

Then, what is faith? ***Hebrews 11:1*** says, *"Now faith is the substance of things hoped for, the evidence of things not seen."*

Romans 10:17 says, *"Faith comes by hearing, and hearing the word of God."*

Hebrews 11:6 tells us, *"But without faith it is impossible to please Him, for he who comes to God must believe that He is, and that He is a rewarder of those who diligently seek Him."*

I was leaving my old ways of thinking, with my mind being cleansed and renewed by God's Word with the help of the Holy Spirit giving me understanding of it all.

I used to verbalise and complain that I did not have enough

money, and for some reason I did not have enough money. There is a warning from **Proverbs 18:21, "Death and life are in the power of the tongue, and those who love it will eat its fruit."**

I could very well say that I was cursing myself with what I declared. When I realised the error of declaring faithless words over my situation, I repented (stopped) of my old way of confession and tried to find out God's Word in the matter instead and then confess that. Then one day I came across **Psalm 23:1-2,** and the Scripture told me there that, **"The Lord is my shepherd; I shall not want. He makes me lie down in green pastures; He leads me beside the still waters. He restores my soul."**

Within this Psalm, God was showing me something new about himself. That helped me to change from the negative words I used to verbalise. Now, instead of complaining I would tell God my needs and ask Him to provide me with them. Scripture says, **"Yet you do not have because you do not ask" (James 4:2).**

Within a very short time, I was put to the test when I had a £50 car tax bill fine and I had no money to pay for it. After praying to the Lord about it and presenting the need of £50 to Him, I left it in His hands and refused to worry about it. A week before I was due to pay the bill, my workmate, who used to travel down the country every Thursday for a meeting, had his car rendered useless from the previous night. He came and asked me to drive him down in my car, so I said yes. That journey meant to me in cash terms the sum of £53, which was paid to me the very day I needed to pay for the car tax. I thanked the Lord for His on-time provision. The Lord tests our faith with little things at first to bring us to a place of faith for larger things later on. The devil, on the other hand, does his utmost to crush and destroy us and kill us if he can, but only if we let him. **James 4:7** instructs us: **"Therefore submit to God, resist the devil and he will flee from you."** The word "therefore" says that there is something that precedes it, so, have a look at it; it will be good for you.

In 1984, my work ended with the engineering company and I was made redundant as the building industry was in crisis. My workmates were anxious for me to get my CV written out and to get it posted to employers before college leavers were out, but I did not feel their anxiety. I felt that self-employment was my direction—in the carpentry line.

A verse in **Romans 8:28** encouraged me, which says, *"And we know that all things work together for good to those who love God, to those who are the called according to His purpose."*

That is a securing promise. I was seeing that when I trust the Lord, He directs me through the Scriptures and that He loves me and wants to prosper me in every way. I gasped and hungered for His Word.

Third John 1:2 says, *"Behold, I pray that you may prosper in all things and be in health, just as your soul prospers."*

Our soul is comprised of our mind, will and emotions. The Word of God opened up to me as I searched for God's direction in **Philippians 4:6-7**. This said, *"Be anxious for nothing, but in everything by prayer and supplication with thanksgiving, let your requests be made known to God; and the peace of God, which surpasses all understanding, will guard your hearts and minds through Christ Jesus."*

When I had read these verses and had prayed to Jesus about my concerns, I was unable to work up any anxiety, and I believed that even though I was told I was no longer needed in the company, the Lord was going to provide me with something. The Lord did provide me with contracts in the carpentry line.

My Discovery of an Everlasting Father

As I said earlier, I looked for a father figure in another older man when my own father died. Six months after coming to the Lord, I realised that that search had come to an end as I found that Father figure through Jesus, that wonderful counsellor, who gave heaps of affirmation, direction, comfort, security, care, and provision.

Do you remember me telling you about the things I treasured in my heart that were not good and kept me from yielding to the Lord? One day it dawned on me that the Lord removed those things from my heart and I did not even notice them gone. He filled me with so many new desires and priorities.

I said at the start of this testimony that I was always talking in school. Well, I still love talking. I am still distracting people— disturbing their false sense of peace by talking to them about Jesus and His Kingdom. At this stage of my life, Jesus is the only worthwhile topic of conversation, because to talk about Him is to give and receive words that pertain to life. Jesus wired me up to talk. As a young man, I talked about many irrelevant things; now I talk about Him. Some things never change.

In *John 6:67-68*, many disciples turned away because the words of Jesus were hard to take and walked with Jesus no more:

> *Then Jesus said to the twelve, "Do you also want to go away?" (verse 67).*

> *But Simon Peter answered Him, "Lord, to whom shall we go? You have the words of eternal life." (verse 68).*

Trying to Decide on my Future Work in Carpentry or Photography

I had a new master now and I was no longer to make serious decisions by leaning on my own understanding. I was to acknowledge Jesus in all my ways and as the next verse promises, He would direct my path through His Word.

I am so blessed with the Scripture. I have to say it again. In *Psalm 119:105,* the Psalmist states, *"Your word is a lamp to my feet and a light to my path."*

I place great reliance and trust in Scripture, I have proven for myself the truth of the above Scripture reference, as you will see throughout my stories.

Back in 1984, I was employed as an architectural draughtsman, but the national economy was on a downturn and I was made redundant—leaving me wondering as to what I was going to proceed with in the area of work.

I had three thoughts:

1. I could go to Saudi Arabia and work long and hard

for a time, come home and build my house without any mortgage.

2. I thought of working as a carpenter.

3. I thought of photography as a job.

One day I was standing outside a friend's front door and I was thinking about the Saudi Arabia job prospect when suddenly I had a vision of a person coming up to me where I was standing and shooting me dead. Life over! With that, I had the thought that I came into the world with nothing and I am going to leave the same way. There are no trailers behind a coffin. I felt the Lord telling me that there was no need to go off to Saudi and that He would supply my needs right here in Galway. Well that was the end of that idea.

I had to decide between carpentry and photography. I weighed the pros and cons for each profession.

I saw that I had more pros for the carpentry, and still I wanted to do photography. Therefore, I had my struggle which had been going on since June 1984, and it was now sometime in August.

Our small church fellowship at the time used to go over to Wales for a week in August for a Bible week. On Wednesday evening of that week, I happened to be at the meeting with my pastor at the time, Graeme Wylie. The preacher came out and before he started preaching, he said, *"Stop being double-minded; the devil has you there and you are going nowhere."*

Graeme, who knew my double-mindedness regarding my work, gave me an elbow in my side and said, "Did you hear that?"

I said, "I did."

However, when I heard the preacher say this, my jaw dropped and I could hardly believe my ears. I heard it, and started to heed it. I knew the Lord wanted me to sort this out finally.

The next day I started reading the Bible with the need to receive the Lord's direction for my future work. As I quoted at the beginning of this story, the Lord directs by His Word.

I happened to read *1 Thessalonians 4,* and when I came to

the *verses 11 to 12,* I knew the Lord spoke to me.

The Scripture said, ***"That you also aspire to lead a quiet life, to mind your own business, and to work with your hands, as we commanded you, that you may walk properly toward those who are outside, and that you may lack nothing."***

I responded, "Thank you, Lord."

In both carpentry and photography, I work with my hands. However, since I had already written down my pros and cons for each profession, I knew it was carpentry! I made up my mind there and then, and became single-minded toward carpentry.

When I was a few years younger and living at home, I would have laboured around in our old house doing a bit of repair work and I must say that I was inclined to injure myself a lot. I did not respect the sharp tools in the way I should have. Therefore, when I told my family that I had made up my mind to work as a carpenter, they saw red. They advised me against it and said, "What about you being accident-prone?"

I replied and said that I believe the Lord is directing me to do carpentry and I am going to make up my mind and trust Him to keep me from major accidents. Twenty-six years later, and nearly at retirement age, I have had no major accidents. The Lord has kept me. I have heard an expression that goes like this: *The Lord will never lead you where His grace cannot keep you.* Just think about that for a moment. I have found this to be true. I strongly recommend that we can trust the Lord Jesus Christ when He directs us.

I was and still am a good singer and musician, and in my early days as a Spirit-filled Christian, I made a gospel tape and thought I might get on the road doing concerts, as well as doing my carpentry.

In March 1989, I gave a gospel concert with a few other men. During the days leading up to it, I was struggling with swollen glands and a sore throat. I sang the concert and consequently lost my voice for two years. My voice did come back but that was the end of that. If I pursued that kind of life it would not have been leading a quiet life.

After that, I did aspire to lead a quiet life, I tended to my own business as a self-employed contractor. I can now say those twenty-six years from when I received that Scripture, I have lived accordingly. My family and I have never been in need to the point of having nothing. Many times, we were down to the wire, but we never had to beg bread. The Lord always provides on time—never early, never late—but always on time. Our faith is always tested.

Chapter 3

Making a List for a Wife and Finding Her

AFTER I made up my mind up as to the career I was about to pursue, I was faced with another great need to pray about and bring before the Lord, and it was wonderful the way He directed me in a wonderful way, as I will explain in this chapter.

Psalm 145:15 says, *"The eyes of all look expectantly to You, and You give them their food in due season."*

There is both milk and meat in the Bible, and that's why we need to read it to be spiritually nourished. He does not reveal everything to us at once, as we would be overwhelmed. Instead, He reveals small portions at any given time, such as when we really need a prayer answered, or when God wants to direct us in some way. As we read a particular verse, He has a way of letting us know that this very Scripture is for us. The same applies when we see a Christian book lying on a stall or a bookshelf. Your eyes rest on it, you see the title, and you know instantly that you need to purchase that book because you know the Lord has something to say to you through it. You buy the book and store it on your bookshelf to read later. Sometimes that book could be there for a few years and all of a sudden you get the urge to read it. At other times you get a book and you know it has to be immediately read.

As it says in the Scripture above, the Lord gives us our food in due season. A year and a half after coming to Christ, I got a book and knew I had to read it without delay. It was called, *The Fourth Dimension,* written by Dr. David Yong-gi Cho.

In his first chapter "Incubation: A Law of Faith, he said:

God will never bring about any of his great works

without coming through your own personal faith. It is taken for granted that you have faith. The Bible says that faith is the substance of things hoped for, a substance which first has a stage of development—of incubation—before its usage can be full and effective, you might now ask "what are the elements needed to make my faith "usable?"[1]

He lists four basic steps in the process of incubation:

1. Envision a clear-cut objective.
2. Have a burning desire.
3. Pray for assurance.
4. Speak the word.

In this chapter, he tells a story about praying to God for a bicycle, a chair and a desk. I will try to condense his story. Dr. Cho said in his book:

I am a man who is greatly impressed with the Word of God and His promises. From Scripture, I knew I was a son of God, a child of the King of Kings and of the Lord of Lords. So why should a son of the King of Kings be in such lack? All I was requiring was a bicycle, a chair and a desk.[2]

He prayed in vague terms for six months and was still in need of those items, even though he had faith to receive them. He was expecting them because in Scriptures God promises to supply his needs according to His riches in glory by Christ Jesus. Still nothing happened.

At this stage I got so frustrated and depressed and argued with God. I could not ask people to exercise their faith when I could not even practice it myself. After a period of weeping and emptying myself, I suddenly felt serenity and a feeling of tranquillity come into my

---

1 David Yonggi Cho, *The Fourth Dimension,* (Alachua, FL: Bridge-Logos Publishers, 1979)
2 Ibid.

soul. Whenever I had that kind of feeling, it was the sense of the presence of God. He always speaks, so I waited. Then that still, small voice welled up in my soul, and the Spirit said, "My Son, I heard your prayer a long time ago." Right away, I blurted out "Then where are my desk, chair and bicycle?"

The Spirit then said, "Yes, that is the trouble with you, and with all my children. They beg me, demanding every kind of request, but they ask in such vague terms that I cannot answer. Don't you know that there are dozens of kinds of desks, chairs and bicycles; but you have simply asked me for a desk, chair and bicycle? You never ordered a specific desk, chair or bicycle."

That was a turning point in my life. I then said, "Lord, do you really want me to pray in definite terms?" This time the Lord led me to turn to Hebrews 11, "Faith is the substance of things, clear-cut things, 'hoped for.'"

So I apologised to the Father and started all over again and was specific about my needs. I gave all the details and became pregnant (expecting) in my spirit for the supply of those items. I went to bed that night full of faith, but when I woke up the next morning all the faith was gone, there was nothing to sustain that faith I said.

On that morning when I was reading the Bible, and looking for a particular Scripture to speak on, suddenly my eyes fell on <u>Romans 4:17, "God raises the dead, and calls those things that be not as if they were."</u> My heart fastened to that Scripture, and it began to boil in my heart. I said to myself, "I might as well call those things which are not as if they were, as if I already had them." I received the answer to the problem of how to keep one's faith.[3]

---

3 Ibid.

Dr. Cho declared to his people that he had the three items, but that brought its own troubles, as they knew he did not have a cent to his name. He was eventually able to explain to them the concept given by the Holy Spirit. He shared what God said:

I'll ask you a few questions. If you can answer my questions, I'll show you all of those things. How long were you in your mother's womb before you were born into this world?

He scratched his head and replied, "Nine months."

"What were you doing for nine months in your mother's womb?"

"Oh, I was growing."

"But no one saw you?"

"No one could see me because I was inside my mother."

"You were as much a baby inside your mother's womb as you were when you were born into this world. You gave me the right answer."

Last evening I knelt down and prayed to the Lord for that desk, chair, and bicycle, and by the power of the Holy Spirit, I conceived that desk, chair, and bicycle. It was as if they were growing inside me. And they were as much a desk, chair, and bicycle as when they would be at the time of their delivery.[4]

You can imagine the laughter that brought—and with it a completely new understanding of faith.

It just takes time, as a mother takes time to give birth to a child. It takes time for you, too, because you become pregnant with all of your clear-out objectives.

I was praising the Lord and sure enough, when the time came, I had every one of those things. I had exactly all the things I had asked for—a desk made out of Philippine mahogany; a chair made from the Japanese Mitsubishi

---

4 Ibid.

Company, with rollers on the tips so that I could roll
around when I sat on it, and a slightly used bicycle,
with gears on the side, from an American missionary's
son. I brought that desk, chair, and bicycle into my house
and I was completely changed in my prayer attitude.[5]

For me, reading the testimony from his book changed my prayer attitude as well.

Dr. Cho had to go through the agony of waiting for six months without assurance in his heart, even though he believed and trusted God for the requested items. God revealed to him that he needed to be specific with Him, which in turn helped him to pray correctly and get his prayers answered.

I did not have to endure the agony that Dr. Cho had to go through in discovering this truth. It goes to show that when we come to a place of desperation, and with a heart seeking for the truth, we will find it. For me, Dr. Cho did all the groundwork. I just had to read his testimony, which showed me the scriptural principles he applied and the result he got.

I knew that the Lord had me reading this for a purpose, instructing me how to walk this walk of faith. I grabbed hold of it. At the time, I was in need of a wife, and his testimony inspired me to be detailed with the specification of a woman who would be my future spouse. I was single at this stage for a few years, as my first marriage had ended in divorce. The psalmist states in *Psalm 37:4,* *"If you delight yourself in the Lord, He will give you the desires of your heart."* I was confident in this Scripture, so when I had the desire for a wife, I knew it was God's desire for me also.

As I sat down one day and put pen to paper, I invited the Holy Spirit to guide me because He knew my heart better than I knew my own heart. There is a directive for us in *Proverbs 3:5-6* which says, *"Trust in the Lord with all your heart, and lean not on your own understanding; in all your ways acknowledge Him,*

---

5 Ibid.

and He shall direct your paths." By applying this Scripture to this situation, how could I go wrong?

To give you an inkling as to how my list went, without being too specific—the priority for me within my specification was the woman had to be filled with the Holy Spirit, knowing and loving the Lord, and desiring prayer.

The Lord gave Adam a helper in Eve. So I agreed with that, and it covered a multitude of items.

My list covered looks, size, age, homemaking qualities, and wanting children—being a good cook was in there, too. She had to be sporting and adventurous, accepting my previous marriage and child situation.

The extensive list I made left no room for doubt. The Holy Spirit was invited to participate with me, and then there was another equation, my personality being detailed. This list was not beyond the perimeters of the Lord's capabilities to provide. I had no doubt about His ability to supply all that I had asked for. Scripture in *Luke 1:37* declares, *"For with God nothing is impossible."* God will never direct you into something that He will not or cannot supply.

It is imperative that we have His directive in every major matter in our lives, especially a marriage partner. Otherwise, we may find ourselves lacking greatly, or else going the wrong direction.

Another directive for us is found in *Psalm 127:1, "Unless the Lord builds the house, they labour in vain who built it; unless the Lord guards the city, the watchmen stays awake in vain."* In other words, the Lord has to be the initiator and director in your venture.

If I had made my list without inviting the Lord to direct me I could very well have asked for all the wrong qualities, and be left regretting it at the end of the day.

If we leave the Lord out of our plans, He leaves us on our own, and then we are left relying on our own wisdom, strength, and provision. This will not benefit us at all.

I compiled my list in October 1984, and it enabled me to envision her, so that when she came across my path I would recognise the Lord's provision for me. I was focused now. I asked the Lord to send her my way, and five months later, He did. In March 1985, a couple within our small assembly got married, so we all went to the wedding. After the meal at the wedding reception, the music and the dancing started, and most of us were out on the floor. I had a few dances early on that evening, where my partner did not have the same rhythm as me, and we would step on each other's toes. Those incidences did not inspire me to continue dancing.

Then I saw a woman who was not dancing, but she had a boyfriend with her. About a year before this, she had come into our prayer meeting one night. When I saw her then, my first thought was, "There is hope yet." But when she was followed in by her boyfriend, I cancelled the thought because she was spoken for. At the wedding, I plucked up the courage and asked her boyfriend if it was okay for me to dance with his woman friend. He gave me the "all clear." When we got on the dance floor and started to waltz around the floor, I was very aware of the fact that we flowed so well together, moving as one person. After a few dances, I gave her back to her boyfriend. I discovered sometime later that this woman's relationship with her boyfriend had ended.

Later on, I got talking to her as we both had a sense of oneness. However, we decided to postpone any progress for many weeks, just to see if God was in this. We did not want our emotions to get the better of us.

After six weeks, we arranged for a dinner date, which gave me the opportunity to ask her a few questions, and to see if she was fulfilling the specifications on my list. The first night confirmed the requests on my list, so we arranged for more meetings.

Within three weeks I discovered that this woman—you have guessed it—Geraldine, fulfilled all the items on my list except two. I knew after three weeks that Geraldine was my wife-to-be and I had hardly even kissed her.

Geraldine was a half an inch shorter than the height I specified, and three years younger than the age I had asked, but these were minor differences in my estimation. In September 1986, we got married and you will read the rest of the story later in the book.

God supplied my need according to His riches in glory by Christ Jesus. That list was not impossible for Him. About a year and a half into our marriage, Geraldine discovered the diary I used for writing my list of qualities I wanted in my future wife. She said she could see herself in it.

Let us not be deceived into thinking that we must have sex before marriage to know if we are suited for each other. When we keep to the Lord's standards and requirements, He will bless us and keep us, and provide us with the best.

The Gift of Faith

It is wonderful how the Lord leads us on from one degree of faith to another. He gives us increase as we are obedient and faithful in the first things He gives us to handle.

In 1985, when I was a very young Spirit-filled Christian, I was in Limerick city attending a week's training in outdoor street evangelism.

We spent most of the week doing our training indoors in one of the schools, and our task at the end of the week was to go downtown to the main street in Limerick and preach to the public with our sketch boards.

The day came for us to go to the main street to do our exam in public. As we were gathering our equipment together to go down centre of the city, the rain came down by the buckets-full. The leader who was teaching us said that we would not bother going down to the city centre. Instead, we would do our exam in the college amongst ourselves.

For some reason I rejected his decision, as I saw this as defeatist. I said, "Where is the power and authority? The authority we are supposed to have in Christ? Where is our faith? There was no victory in this decision. This does not rest correctly in my spirit. We trained all week indoors to preach to the people outdoors."

Faith rose up within me and I overruled the leader. I declared that it was not going to rain and that we were going to proceed to go to the city centre.

The Lord was in it because the leader replied, "Okay, let's go." We packed all our gear into the car in the rain. We climbed into our cars ourselves and proceeded to drive to the city centre.

When we arrived at our destination, you guessed it. The rain stopped, the leader was speechless, we got to preach, and 3,000 people were saved!

There are times in our lives when God gives us a gift of faith for a certain thing. We cannot explain it—we just have it. So speak it out, declare it. Move on it and see all Heaven back us up.

The leader that day got a lesson in rising up in the Spirit and declaring by faith to the elements (the rain in this case) to be removed.

The spiritual, unseen world to the naked eye is always dominant over the physical, material world. Therefore, it is imperative for us to live by faith because it is God's language. If we want Him to work with us, we need to talk His language. ***"But without faith it is impossible to please Him..." (Hebrews 11:6).*** I was beginning to realise that God was doing something new in me. He was giving me a gift of faith. This is a supernatural ability to believe God without any doubting.

Request for a Workshop

I have found out for myself that to be in a place of frustration and discomfort can be a very good place to be. It brings us to a place of decision, and hopefully we turn to the Lord in that condition. Something has to happen!

Applying the same scriptural principle that Dr. Cho used in prayer for his bicycle, chair, and desk, I was specific in my prayer for a wife, and the Lord answered my requests. Therefore, I continued to be specific in prayer in my search for a workshop, which I badly needed.

I had just started working in my carpentry business making small bits of furniture. I was putting these bits of furniture together in the small three-foot-wide corridor of my home. We had sheds, but they had no roofs on them in those years, which meant I could not work in them. With every job, the dust was piling up, and it was getting intolerable. Something had to happen. One day, I got several cheques as deposits for small jobs, so I had to move. That night I went before God and started writing down the details of a workshop that I thought would fit what I needed. I stated that I needed:

1. An 800-foot square workshop
2. It to be in the town
3. To be beside a timber yard
4. My own entrance
5. A twelve-foot square sliding door and
6. Rent that I could afford

On that Tuesday night, I said to the Lord, "I'm going out tomorrow and I'm going to do two things—first, to buy some material for jobs, and next, to look for the workshop that I requested."

My first port of call was a timber yard. I liked the way they treated their material there. As I was walking through the premises, a thought came to me that there must be some place in this complex that is not utilised. At that moment, I did not pay any more attention to it. **Psalm 23:2** states, *"He [God] **makes me to lie down in green pastures.**"* I went to the office and asked if they had a particular type of timber. It was out of supply, so I went around to all the other timber yards in town, but no one had the material I needed. It was a very frustrating day. In the early afternoon, I found myself back in the first timber yard. I changed my mind about the material I needed to use for the job.

Now, this time I did something about that thought I had had earlier that morning, when I was walking through the premises. I have found that it may be beneficial to take note of where you are when you get thoughts, just as I did, especially after you have prayed to God. It might be the place of God's answer.

In any case, I asked the man behind the desk if he knew of any area in the complex not being utilised. He thought for a moment and said that a mechanic's workshop had been lying idle for some time. He asked, "Don't you know the boss?" I said I did, so he said the best thing to do is to go to him and have a chat.

Without further ado, I left the yard and went to talk to the boss. When I presented my request to him, his reply was, "God works in mysterious ways." That sounded good to my ears.

I told the boss what I needed and said that the man in the office told me to come to him and present my request. The boss told me to come back next week. I replied, "That is too long to wait. I need to get going, as I know what I need and I just want you to tell me if you have a place that fits my bill."

He said, "Okay, come back to me tomorrow morning and I'll have a look in the meantime."

Thursday morning I rose up, prayed, and read my Bible.

In *Psalm 119:105,* the psalmist states, *"Your word is a lamp to my feet and a light to my path."*

That morning I read *Psalm 31* and when I came to *verse 8,* it said, *"You have set my feet in a wide place."* When I read that verse, I knew that God had spoken to me because when God speaks to us, He alerts us. We wake up and pay attention to it. He gives us the knowing that this Word is the answer to the particular prayer request we have made.

We would be very foolish not to obey it. I hope this explanation helps you in knowing when God speaks to you. It is not a spooky thing, but is very practical.

"Faith comes by hearing and hearing the word of God" (Romans 10:17).

I return to the story. When I read *Psalm 31:8,* faith rose up within me and I knew that the workshop was coming. I was pregnant in my spirit with the workshop. You may laugh, but that is the reality of it. I was in a state of expectation.

I went to the boss later that morning and he said he had both bad news and good news for me. We proceeded to go up to the timber yard.

You have to believe what happened next. We passed by the entrance to the main timber yard, walked up the road about seventy-five metres, and went down a lane to a shed, which had its own entrance. The shed was 800-foot square had sliding doors twelve-foot square, in town, and he gave it to me at a rent I could afford. He was God's answer to my prayer request, and I was God's answer to his prayer request.

Psalm 23:1-2 says ***"The Lord is my Shepherd, I shall not want, He makes me to lie down in green pastures; He leads me beside the still waters."***

I was in the process of seeing how great a provider my heavenly Father was to me. I had that workshop for many years until circumstances changed around me, but the Lord kept providing for me through a married couple who let me work in their unused garage. God is good all the time.

Finding our First Home

As we made plans for our wedding, we had to pray and commit to the Lord the whole question of our new home. Where were we going to live? How much were we able to spend? What kind of a house did we desire? What size of family did we want? Do we look for an older house or a new house? It was a wonderful and exciting project.

One morning while I was praying, I felt the Lord prompting me to write down the specifics of the house that I desired. At one time, Geraldine was working out of town. I rang her during lunch and told her that I felt the Lord prompting me to write down the details of the house that I desired. She replied that she could hardly believe her ears because as she was driving to her work that morning, the Lord spoke to her as well to write down the details of the house she desired. There we were; the two of us on the same page! The Lord spoke to us at both the same time, and it was time to put pen to paper. Separately, we wrote down the details of what we desired in a house so we could test what was in each other's hearts, without influencing one another.

When we examined each other's list—would you believe it?—we had the same house in our hearts. I was a bit more detailed in my list, of course. You would never have guessed that now, would you!

We wanted a four-bedroom house, detached. As I had a workshop in town already, I put down that our house needed to be within a one and a half-mile radius of the workshop.

We started looking at previously-owned houses because we thought that they would be cheaper than a new house. We looked everywhere within the one and a half-mile radius of the workshop. Then somebody told us that we should change our thinking from a secondhand house to a new house because the government was giving a £3000 mortgage subsidy and £2000 grant to first-time buyers. That was a total of £5000 available to us. Therefore, we started looking for new houses within the same radius of the workshop. I wanted a new house where the block work had just begun, as I could look at the plans and alter some aspects of the house design internally before anything began. That narrowed the prospects down a good bit.

Proverbs 16:9 says, *"A man's heart plans his way, but the Lord directs his footsteps."*

Yes, the Lord requires us to think and plan, and once we have done that, we ask Him to direct our footsteps.

One Sunday afternoon, off we went on our house hunt and to our amazement, we came across a semi-circle of houses, about nine in all, and all at various stages of construction. There were two houses in the middle of the row that were at a very early stage of construction, but we had to wait until the next day to find out if they were still for sale.

We went down to the auctioneer who was selling the houses and inquired if the two least built houses in the middle were still unsold in his books. He rang the contractor to inquire if he had the same story. He said to the auctioneer that he had sold one of them and the only one that was left was the one that was least built. God is so good. We told the auctioneer to hold that house for us and that we would have the deposit for him by Friday.

At this time, Geraldine was working in the bank as relief staff, which meant each morning she went to work, she never knew where she was going to be sent or for how long. This, for me, was absolute horror as I was still gripped with fear, suspicion, and mistrust. Nevertheless, even through that we kept moving forward and making plans for the future together. I could not be married to her while she was working on relief staff. I was too insecure.

Friday morning came and we went down to put our deposit on the house in fear and trembling. Later that day, Geraldine got a letter from the bank—and guess what? She was made a permanent staff member in the local branch downtown. Faith is surely tested. I was so grateful and thankful to my Lord *"... who will not allow you to be tempted beyond what you are able, but with the trial will also make the way of escape that you may be able to bear it (1 Corinthians 10:13).*

Did you ever get the sense that the Lord is for you every step of the way? He is going ahead of you and preparing the way as *Psalm 23:1-3* says, *"The Lord is my Shepherd; I shall not want, He makes me to lie down in green pastures, He leads me beside the still waters, He restores my soul. He leads me in the path of righteousness, for His name's sake."*

The house that we found was a four-bedroom, detached house within one and a half-mile radius of my workshop. This is another example of visualising something and having the Lord direct you. He goes before you and you, just need to follow Him.

Chapter 4

God's Healing and Deliverance From Fear and Mistrust

ARISING out of previous relationships I'd had, and having observed how people mistreat each other, my mind was not in a good place. As a single man again for a good number of years and not in any committed relationship, I thought my emotions were in good shape and that my past negative experiences were dead and buried. But I was about to discover something different.

Realising that Geraldine was to become my wife and understanding fully the seriousness of it, I suddenly became aware of the feelings of fear, mistrust, suspicion, and insecurity. I was in an awful condition. I wanted to walk away. In fact, I was in prison because of my negative emotions, and I thought the only way to freedom was to walk away from this relationship. However, to walk away would only have brought defeat and would have deprived me of a marriage that I greatly needed.

2 Timothy 1:7 says, *"For God has not given us a spirit of fear, but of power and of love and of sound mind."*

So where did this fear come from? Well, I realised I had built up strongholds in my soul from past hurts and traumas that brought about:

Wrong attitudes, wrong patterns of thinking, wrong ideas, wrong desires, wrong beliefs, wrong habits and wrong behaviours learned from ungodly sources. A stronghold is anything you rely upon to defend your opinion and position, even if you are dead wrong. Strongholds protect these patterns of thinking, giving the devil opportunities to twist and distort them even further.[6]

Jesus described the devil as a thief who has come to destroy, steal, and kill.

Because of my past hurts, the devil was having a field day with me, distorting and twisting my thoughts and emotions. I know all this now because the Scriptures reveal that unseen spiritual activities are at work. But at that time, I was very ignorant of the forces at work against me. All I knew was that I was gripped with fear, and I thought I had no power over it. When I was in the midst of it, my mind was unable to think straight. The one thing that kept Geraldine and me together was the fact that we both knew that the Lord had put us together, which brought us through this storm.

Fear, suspicion, and mistrust would take over me if Geraldine ever smiled or talked to another man. I would interrogate her as if she had committed a crime. The poor woman, who was the friendliest person in the world, could not exhibit any of her wonderful qualities because of my intimidation.

The fact was, I was in prison and there was no way Geraldine was going to live outside prison while I was inside.

I had visions and dreams of her doing unfaithful acts behind my back, and nobody could ever convince me that they were incorrect. Our relationship was under great strain.

When we have a spirit of fear working against us in our lives, it is horrific what that spirit flings at us.

However, in spite of all this going on, we continued to make plans for marriage—plans to buy our new home—because we knew the Lord had put us together.

We eventually got married in September 1986, but that spirit of fear, along with my mind playing tricks, was still trying to destroy our relationship.

Geraldine was becoming more worn out with my accusations

---

6 Liberty Savard, *Shattering Your Strongholds,* (Alachua, FL: Bridge-Logos Publishers, 1992)

month in and month out, until about twelve months into our marriage. We came home one day after visiting the city and it must have been one of those days when I was again accusing her. There was never any physical abuse, however. When we came to our home, Geraldine went up to the bedroom and I went into the kitchen. Even though I was thinking and saying nasty things to her, I was in an awful condition and hated myself for it. While in the kitchen, I heard a knock on the ceiling coming from our bedroom floor. When I went upstairs to talk with Geraldine, the Lord opened my eyes and showed me the horror of what I had said to Geraldine, and the toll it was having on her life.

I immediately repented of (turned away from) my verbal abuse that I inflicted upon her. I repented to the Lord for all I had said. I told God and Geraldine that I would never, ever, say those things I used to say ever again. I received forgiveness from both God and my wife.

The Lord blessed us with twenty-one additional years of marriage until Geraldine died of cancer in 2008. In those twenty-one years, I never ever again said what I used to say to her. From that day of repentance, the Lord restored to us what was robbed from us in our two and a half years of courtship and marriage. It was as if the Lord had glued us together. We were at one with each other and inseparable. Our marriage was blissful, and many people can testify to that.

Geraldine could now look at another man and even embrace one if the situation arose, and I was at peace. The destructive thinking pattern was finished, and the Lord transformed my thinking through believing the Scriptures, which brought about correct thinking. Furthermore, I was beginning to receive the perfect love from God and Geraldine. Scripture says perfect love casts out fear.

The Lord restored to us—and to me primarily—His peace and His love. I could trust again. The Lord delivered me out of captivity and all that went with it, and into freedom and security.

1 John 4:18-19 states, ***"There is no fear in love; but perfect love casts out fear, because fear involves torment. But he who fears has not been made perfect in love. We love Him because He first loved us."***

People who operated with prophetic gifting would often come to our church. Whenever they spoke over Geraldine and me, they would say that God had uniquely put us together and we were joined at the hip. Those people would not have known one single thing about us before meeting us that day.

Six months after I repented to Geraldine and the Lord, I saw those imaginations that I used to have of Geraldine, fading away, going back to where they belonged. I was horrified at what I used to think about, and how I used to accuse.

I hear people say that time heals, but I cannot agree with that statement after what I have gone through.

Jesus Christ heals and uses situations over time to confront us about the condition of our heart and our need for His touch on our lives. God loves us the way we are, but He loves us too much to leave us in our present state. He wants to transform us bit by bit into the image of His Son, Jesus. This is possible by our willingness to surrender to the Lord, and when we do, the Holy Spirit does the rest.

When Geraldine came to the end of what she was taking from me, the Lord stepped in. Many times, we have to get to the place where we say, "I can't stand it any longer." Whenever anybody cries out to the Lord for help, he or she will receive it. He will never encroach into our lives without us first asking for help because He has set the boundary line of free will in place. He will not come to our help until asked. Therefore, we should not blame God for our troubles when He has been left out of them.

Examine your habits:

2 Kings 17:34 says, ***"God said... they continue practising former [habits]; they do not fear the Lord, nor do they follow... the law...which the Lord...commanded..."***

Understand this: any habit you feed will strengthen its grip on your life. Ask anyone recovering from addiction; we only become willing to change when we hit the bottom. Prodigals do not come home until they have lost everything! However, that does not have to be your story. Your heavenly Father is waiting to welcome you back. You are a child of the Most High—captivity is unnatural to you. You will never be free until you despise your chains. Whether you're bound by a substance, a relationship or a life that's out of order, you're circumstances won't change until your mind is released from the grip of old thought patterns and renewed by God's Word (Romans 12:2), so start putting in place new habits, for what you do consistently you become permanently. Begin the Bible-reading habit. Put it first on your "to do list" or you will not do it faithfully! ... Those who discover these words, live, really live... Proverbs 4:22. Set a specific time for prayer, otherwise everything else will crowd it out. In prayer, God will tell you how He feels about things. Can you afford to live without His impact? Attend church regularly, support it with your finances, exercise your spiritual gifts and begin to invest time and energy into relationships that sharpen and strengthen you spiritually. God will say things to you in His house that He will not say anywhere else. Your daily habits are carving out an irresistible future. If you want to know where you're headed—examine them![7]

There is a wonderful promise in the New Testament in *1 Corinthians 10:13:*

No temptation [can mean trial as well] has overtaken you except such as is common to man; but God is faithful, who will not allow you to be tempted beyond what you are able, but with the temptation [trial] will also make

---

7 UCB (United Christian Broadcasting) Word for Today booklet, 8th January 2011. Hanchurch Christian Centre, Hanchurch Lane, Stoke-on-Trent, ST48RY.

the way to escape, that you may be able to bear it.

We saw the Lord's faithfulness to His Word in this Scripture, which was still applicable in later years when we were in the midst of other trials. When something got too much for us, we would see the deliverance that the Lord brings.

I want to say that God had put special steel in Geraldine's backbone to withstand the verbal onslaught she got from me in the beginning.

I have discovered that repenting to the Lord about our sinful state brings about His redeeming quality, deliverance, and freedom.

The mistrust that possessed me predated my first marriage. I had a trust issue until God set me free as described in Chapter 2. It was very important to get God's perspective on the husband and wife relationship so that my old destructive thinking patterns would not have victory over me again. To make sure that would not happen, it was important for us to find out from the Bible what God had to say on this matter. We need to conduct our married life in the way God instructed, and thus out of obedience to His Word we would experience His peace.

We discovered from **Ephesians 5:22-32** that marriage is sacred to God. It shows us that there is a great parallel between Christ (the bridegroom) and the Church (His bride) and the marriage between husband and wife. Marriage is God's order for a relationship between a man and a woman.

I experienced a marriage breakup, which was born out of my destructive sinful nature. It was still affecting my courtship and the start of my second marriage. The heartbreak and devastation, which was brought upon everyone connected to it, was not yet healed.

I don't want any of you who are about to get married, or are married already, to go through what I went through. I want to assure you that there is hope for you. Can I share with you what we discovered in the Bible and lived out in our marriage? There were instructions in regard to our roles in marriage, and how we should treat each other. We obeyed these instructions to the best of our abilities with the desire to obey the Lord. We lived in such harmony and peace; we prospered and bore much fruit. My only regret is that I did not have the Lord ruling my life, or the knowledge of the Scriptures directing and teaching me how to live during my first marriage. From my perspective, Geraldine did not have the behavioural problems I had. These scriptural principles seemed instilled in her already. I was a work in progress, and still am!

Much of what we learned came from *Ephesians 5:22-32*:

Family order, the specific instructions that the Apostle Paul gives to husbands and wives are a glimpse of the bridegroom and bride—a heavenly model for every marriage on Earth.

As a husband, how should I behave toward my wife? Look to Christ, the divine bridegroom, in his relationship with the church; love her, sacrifice for her, listen to her concerns, take care of her, be as sensitive to her needs and her hurts as you are to those of your own body.

As a wife, how should I behave towards my husband? Look to the chosen bride, the Church. In its relationship with Christ; respect him, acknowledge his calling as head of the family, respond to his leadership, listen to him, praise him, be unified in purpose and will with him; be a true helper (See Genesis 2:18).

No husband and wife can do this by mere willpower or resolve, but since you (including your marriage) are "His workmanship" (Eph. 2:8-10), God will help bring this about. Look at 1 Corinthians 11:3: 1 Peter 3:1-7.[8]

Notes: Concerning Scripture in 1 Peter 3:1:

A word of wisdom to wives, women. The spirit of submission, whereby a woman voluntarily acknowledges her husband's leadership responsibility under God, is an

---

8 Notes from Spirit-Filled Life ® Bible.

act of faith. The Bible nowhere "submits" or subordinates women to men, generically. However, this text calls a woman to submit herself to her husband (Eph. 5:22), and the husband is charged to lovingly give himself to caring for his wife—never exploiting the trust of her submission (Eph. 5:25-29). This divinely ordered arrangement is never shown, nor was it ever given, to reduce the potential, purpose, or fulfilment of the woman. Only fallen nature or persistent church traditionalism, finding occasion through "proof texts" separated from their biblical context, can make a case for the social exploitation of women or the restriction of women from church ministry.

1 Timothy 2:12 and 1 Corinthians 14:34-35, which disallows a woman's teaching (in an unwelcomed manner). Usurping authority, or creating a nuisance by public argument, all relate to a woman's relationship with her husband. (The Greek word for man in 1 Tim. 2:12 is "aner," which is a readily translated "husband." The context clearly recommends "husband" as does the evidence of the rest of the NT related to the viability of a woman's public voice in Christian assemblies.)

The Bible's word of wisdom to women seems to be summarized in Peter's word here; counsel given to a woman whose husband is an unbeliever. She is told that her "words" are not the key to success in winning her husband to Christ; but her Christ-like, loving spirit is. Similarly, this wisdom would apply to any woman with the potential for a public ministry of leadership in the church. Her place will most likely be given when she is not argumentatively insistent upon it; so much is given to "winning" it by gracious, loving, and servant like spirit—the same spirit that ought to be evident in the life of a man who would lead.

(See Acts 21:9, Genesis 4:25).

Further notes taken from Scripture: 1 Peter 3:1-7,

attitudes toward God determine attitudes toward mates and family order.

Our attitudes toward our mates are governed by our attitudes toward God. A husband may fall short of a wife's expectations and of God's idea of a husband. Nevertheless, she seeks in every way to be a good wife, modelling her behaviour on Christ, who obeyed and trusted the Father even when His own people rejected Him (John 1:11), or, a wife may disappoint her husband, disregard his authority, or withhold her respect. Nevertheless, a husband honours his wife, cares for her, and prays for her, modelling his behaviour on the Father, who "knows our frame" (Psalm 103:14).

Look also at Ephesians 5:22-23 and Colossians 3:18, 19, 23, and 24.[9]

Consider the following list of temptations the enemy of our souls throws at all of us to keep us from doing what is right before our God.

Addressing the worldwide convention of demons, Satan told them: As long as Christians stay close to God we've no power over them, so:

Keep them busy with non-essentials.
1. *Tempt them to overspend and go into debt.*
2. *Make them work long hours to maintain empty lifestyles.*
3. *Discourage them from spending family time, for when homes disintegrate there is no refuge from work.*
4. *Over stimulate their minds with television and computers so that they cannot hear God speaking to them.*
5. *Fill their coffee tables and nightstands with newspapers and magazines so they have no time for Bible reading.*
6. *Flood their letterboxes with sweepstakes, promotions and get-rich-quick schemes; keep*

---

9 Ibid.

them chasing material things.

7. *Put glamorous models on TV and on magazine covers to keep them focused on outward appearances; that way they will be dissatisfied with themselves and their mates.*

8. *Make sure couples are too exhausted for physical intimacy so they will be tempted to look elsewhere.*

9. *Emphasize Santa and the Easter bunny; that way you will divert them from the real meaning of the holidays.*

10. *Involve them in "good" causes so they will not have any time for eternal ones.*

11. *Make them self-sufficient. Keep them so busy working in their own strength that they will never know the joy of God's power working through them.*

12. *Do these 12 things faithfully. I promise—it will work! Have you figured out the difference between being busy and being successful in what God has called you to do? Sometimes being b-u-s-y just means Being Under Satan's Yoke!*[10]

I hope and pray that the notes relating to the various Scriptures that I gave you are helpful.

I hope you will see the reality of what Satan throws at humanity. He wants to distract non-Christians away from God and derail Christians off their walk with God. Satan's nature is one of a thief who comes to destroy, steal and kill, but Jesus has come to give life and life to the full.

Can you see the destructive force of Satan against humanity? Very subtle, but very effective. However, *James 4:6-7* says, *"God resists the proud but gives grace to the humble, therefore submit to God, resist the devil and he will flee from you."*

The devil wants to destroy, steal from, and kill humankind because we are made in God's image and likeness. Satan is also against

---

10 UCB (United Christian Broadcasting) Word for Today booklet, 2 December, 2010. Hanchurch Christian Centre, Hanchurch Lane, Stoke-on-Trent, ST48RY.

marriage. He is working tirelessly at breaking up as many marriages as he can because marriage is sacred to God. The family unit is being broken apart, and children from that marriage are left in a very insecure environment, many times left abandoned and rejected. This brings all sorts of problems when the father is gone. As a result, children can and do end up being angry, rebellious, feeling rejected, and unloved. Growing up without a father's affirmation and secure boundary lines makes them fearful. The unfortunate mother then is left trying to cope with everything, and her *no* to their demands turns to *yes* because she has no energy left. When the children recognise the procedure of getting what they want, they proceed with their relentless pestering bringing about their demands. This brings disorder to the household and nulifies the kingdom of God. ***Righteousness, peace and joy in the Holy Spirit (Romans 14:17)*** is gone out the window. The spiritual consequences of a father abandoning his children, or a father who is never there when they need him, makes it very difficult for the children to put their trust in the heavenly Father through the Lord Jesus Christ.

Another consequence that can happen out of deep hurt and trauma is when we verbalise or internalise negative vows. For example, if a first marriage failed, we can make a vow that we will never get married again. Thus, we imprison ourselves and prohibit ourselves from achieving God's best for us. The power of the tongue can put us in prison and keep us from reaching the full potential that God has for us.

We will only find salvation, freedom, healing, restoration, deliverance, and forgiveness of sins when we repent of our sinful ways. If we surrender our will to Jesus, and accept His perfect sacrifice on the Cross, a great promise in the Bible awaits us. ***"… if God perhaps will grant them repentance, so that they may know the truth, and that they may come to their senses and escape the snare of the devil, having been taken captive by him to do his will" (2 Timothy 2:25-26).***

God Confirming to Me My Son Was Healthy

I have discovered that whatever concerns me or you, concerns God. With the birth of my first child, Matthew, with Geraldine, I was concerned—as everybody is with his or her first child—about the well-being of his physical health. I brought it before the Lord and asked Him to speak to me as to what his condition might be.

It did not take too long before He spoke to me, as I was diligent in the pursuit of the answer. When I was reading *James 1*, as soon as I reached *verse 17*, the Lord answered me and confirmed to me that Matthew was perfect. Here is the way in which I came to that conclusion:

As the name Matthew means "gift of God," *verse 17* says, *"Every good gift and every perfect gift is from above, and comes down from the Father of lights, with whom there is no variation or shadow of turning."*

When reading this verse I had that inner knowing, or the faith, that the Lord had told me I had nothing to worry about in regard to Matthew's physical health. He would be perfect.

As Matthew's name means "gift of God," and in this verse the words used "good gift," and "perfect gift," I took it as a confirmation that Matthew was fine, and with that the Lord quieted my soul. In fact, Matthew was all right.

The Lord directs us in *Philippians 4:6, "Be anxious for nothing, but in everything by prayer and supplication, with thanksgiving, let your requests be made known to God; and the peace of God, which surpasses all understanding, will guard your hearts and minds through Christ Jesus."* Therefore, I did what the Lord instructs in this verse. I brought my anxious thoughts to Him and He answered and gave me His peace.

The Return of Marc to Me in Ireland

After the breakup of my first marriage, Marc's mother got legal custody of him and he went to live with her in England. When he was old enough to fly on his own, he came to live with me every school holiday.

When Marc turned ten, I felt it was time or the season for my son to be under his dad's care. The Lord stirred my heart and I felt Him prompting me to pray for Marc's return to me on a permanent basis. In my prayer to Him, I said that He would need to orchestrate an event that would cause that to happen.

If I started putting the wheels in motion, according to my wisdom and in my timing and way, leaving the Lord out of the situation, I probably would have made an ugly mess of it. I took my hands off it and let the Lord orchestrate the event His way and in His time.

One year later, while Marc was with me during the school summer holidays, word came that Marc's mother and her husband had work in Scotland and the house they were trying to sell in Brighton fell through at the last minute. They suggested that Marc stay here in Ireland for a year while his mother and her husband got themselves settled in Scotland. With everybody in agreement, I knew in my heart that the Lord was orchestrating the event I had prayed. I got him into a good school and he was at the right age to start his secondary schooling from year one to the fifth year in Ireland.

I trusted the Lord that the timing of his coming under my wing was the right time, as he loved me and needed to see the role model of his father worked out. As Marc's father, I could see that the Lord was concerned for Marc and had his best welfare at heart.

Here again, I am reminded how God requires us to pray back to Him the things that He prompts us with because He makes all things beautiful in its time. It is important not to miss His prompting to pray as He responds to our prayers and He sees all things.

Little Marc, on the other hand, who was in the middle of all this, had a lot to cope with. There was no time for him to prepare himself for this change. His rhythm of life was thrown out of balance by not going back to England to be with his mother, and have familiar school friends, who are so important at that age. It left him in shock, bewildered, confused, upset, and disappointed in not going back to England and the life he had there. He was moving between two countries, two cultures, and two family situations. Now he was in another school with children who were total strangers to him and who had a very different mindset to him. On top of that, he had a new language to cope with.

It was a time of readjustment for everybody, but God did not leave Marc without a mother figure. He gave Marc a wonderful stepmother, Geraldine, my new wife who loved him as if he was her own son.

At any given time, we are not fully aware of the full plan that God has for us. We do not see the end of the matter as He does. We just have to trust Him that He knows what He is doing. It is only in hindsight when events have come to their conclusion that we understand fully the plan that God had in the first place.

The Lord's timing is perfect. The Scriptures state to us in *Ecclesiastes 3:11a, "He has made everything beautiful in its time."* We just need to recognise the season we are in and the prompting of the Lord.

As a young man, Marc immigrated to Australia where he has a successful business and a lovely wife, Karen, and between them are the proud parents of a lovely son, Kian. I am a very proud father and grandpa.

The Lord's Directive for our Provision Over Several Christmases

One particular Christmas in the early 1990s, we thought we had bought everything in the food line for the few days over Christmas. We discovered about a half an hour before the shops closed that we were without some cream and one type of vegetable—but we had run out of money also. My sister knocked on our door and said that she was able to get all her food. She had a gift voucher for one of the major food stores left over and asked us if we were in need of it. We replied with a resounding *yes* as we had just discovered we were out of needed ingredients and had no money to buy them. We accepted her voucher with thanks and raced down to the store just in time.

It never ceases to amaze me how the Lord has His eye forever on the little details of our lives, and how He directed my sister to us with that little food voucher.

Thankfully, we got through those few days of Christmas with everybody in the house well-fed and satisfied. But sadly, the food we consumed came to an end, and we needed more money to buy more food.

During this season of our lives, we operated a Bed & Breakfast business, and the guests were not knocking on our door at all. We were located off the main road so we would get very few passers-by at this time of year. We were not long operating the business, and we had no build-up of guests.

Nevertheless, we told our everlasting Father, who is always mindful of us, that we were in need of money for more food. Out of nowhere two guests arrived at our door, asking us if our Bed & Breakfast was open for business. They knew of another Bed & Breakfast up the road, but they were not open for business over the Christmas season. Even if we were not open, we were open now, as we recognised the Lord's provision. We received £28 from the two women for one night's accommodation. We thought we were rich. That satisfied us until I was able to get back at my own maintenance work at the start of the New Year.

Christmas in the Late 1980s

This Christmas we had no money again, and I had no work at hand, as everybody was in need of spending their money on Christmas expenses. I cried out to the Lord and asked Him to help me, and open a door so that I could get the finances we needed to tie us over the Christmas season.

I had a workshop in those days and I worked on many carpentry projects. When you get timber in for a job, there are always spare bits of timber left over. It is very rarely that you would use up every bit of timber bought for any one job. This meant that I had a big pile of odds and ends of old timber stuck in a corner of my workshop—always hoping to be able to use some of the old bits for a new job. It rarely ever happens! The old bits never fitted or suited any new job.

I found myself in the workshop wondering if there was anything I could make to sell out of all spare timber I had in the corner. All of a sudden the Lord gave me an idea. I could chop up all the timber into small pieces to fit into a fireplace, then get large coal bags and fill them up with the pieces of chopped timber.

I did just that and when I had finished, I brought two of my sons with me. We filled the boot of the car with the bags and drove around to as many housing estates as we could to get them all sold. We got the job completed just in time to buy our Christmas supplies. These were in our early days of marriage, when we were at the pin of our collar financially to make ends meet.

Another Christmas in the Late 1980s

Again, I was in need of my heavenly Father to guide and provide for me. I never expected gifts of money to come in through the letterbox of my house, but through my job because I loved to work.

I was visiting my local bank one day, and I was talking to the bank manager about cash flow for my business. Sometimes I would pay for the materials for a job out of my own money, instead of getting a deposit from the person who wanted the work done. Many of my jobs were small, and the amount of money needed to get the materials wasn't that much. Even so, the money was coming out of my own pocket.

The manager suggested that I should use my credit card to buy the materials. By using that method, I would have four to five weeks at my disposal before I would need to pay the money back. By that time my jobs would have been finished and paid for, whereby I would have the money to pay the credit card bill without any need to pay interest.

Upon hearing the manager's suggestion about the credit card, I knew the Lord had given me the wisdom needed to buy all our needs for the Christmas.

That Christmas I bought all that we needed, but not all we wanted, because the Scriptures tell us in **Philippians 4:19 "And my God shall supply all your needs according to His riches in glory by Christ Jesus."** So I obeyed that because I did not have faith for God to supply our wants. We still had a great Christmas.

Christmas and New Year came and went, and I was very mindful that nearly two weeks had passed since I had used the credit card. I really needed work to come in finish I could accomplish the work in time to be paid in advance of the credit card appearing before me. This was on a Thursday, and I cried out to the Lord because I was getting a little desperate.

God does hear the cry of His children because the next day three people came and gave me deposits for jobs they wanted done. I was grateful to the Lord for His care for my family and me, and I was beginning to rest more in His faithfulness.

James 4:2 tells us, **"Yet you do not have because you do not ask."**

I spoke to someone not too long ago who was in need of help from the Lord. I said to the person, "Do you ever draw close to the Lord and tell Him your needs?"

The person replied, "Well, He knows what I need."

I said, "Yes He does, but He won't help you unless you ask Him and invite Him into your situation."

God wants us to seek His face more than His hand of provision. If we did that, we might not have as many problems because seeking His face allows Him to change our character and become more like Him, which brings less trouble on ourselves.

We had another situation concerning food, but not at Christmas time. It was in the early to mid-1990s, and again we were running out of food and had no money. The phone rang and a close friend of ours called us unexpectedly to ask how we were. Geraldine said we were okay, but she did not want to say how we were really doing, as we did not want to sound like we were begging. We wanted the Lord to inspire people, rather than have us telling sob stories. However, after that short conversation ended, the friend rang again and asked strongly, "How are you really doing?" The Lord must have stirred him in his heart. This time Geraldine told him that we had no food in the house. He said, "Give me a half an hour because I am coming up to you."

He was true to his word. He came with a big basket of food and gave us a few pounds as well.

In Psalm 37:25, King David said, *"I have been young, and now am old; yet I have not seen the righteous forsaken, nor His descendants begging bread."*

We surely have seen and tasted that the Lord is good. He moves people with compassion to bless others.

A Friend's Son Healed of Asthma

Psalm 37:23 says, *"The steps of a good man are ordered by the Lord, and He delights in his way."*

I have been aware for a good few years that I am an adopted child of God, filled with the Holy Spirit. I live not for myself primarily, but for Christ Jesus. I am called to live for His purposes, for His will to be done, to be a light in a dark place, to be as salt, and to be His ambassador who represents His ruling authority.

2 Corinthians 5:20-21 says, *"Now then, we are ambassadors for Christ, as though God were pleading through us: we implore you on Christ's behalf, be reconciled to God. For He made Him* [Jesus] *who knew no sin to be sin for us, that we might become the righteousness of God in Him."*

With that in mind, I am always mindful of where the Lord brings me, and if He is opening a door in somebody's heart for the entrance of the gospel (His good news). I know there are no accidents in Christ, so the Lord has a plan and a purpose in everything. I am mindful to be aware of His purposes, and I am always ready to do whatever He is opening up before me or showing me. The Lord's Prayer in *Luke 11:2* says, *"Your kingdom come. Your will be done on earth as it is in heaven."* I do my utmost to make sure that my life gives glory to God and that my life is not an obstacle to others.

The story I am about to tell prompts me to share the Scriptures and commentary to let you know that I am not living my life out of some funny notions.

Many years ago, a woman contacted me to go to her house, which needed a lot of repair work done to it. I discovered that the woman of the house had a love for the Lord and the things of God, but her husband and children were not in the same place spiritually.

Whenever an opportunity arose during break time to talk about the Lord or the Bible, I would encourage the woman in the Lord by sharing the promises of God and scriptural principles to live by. After being there over a period of time, the woman told me that the first day I walked in the front door, her husband had said to her that there was something different about that man. I had not even spoken a word about Christ at this stage. Sometimes we never know what kind of effect we are having on people. The little jobs the woman needed done kept coming back to me, and so did spiritual opportunities.

One Christmas an urgent job needed to be done in one of the bedrooms, so I went there late morning time, thinking everybody would be up. The woman of the house was the only one awake, so we talked again about the Lord. During the course of conversation, she said that one of her sons suffered from asthma and she was concerned about him. I had a quick mental exchange with the Lord and said that if this particular boy comes down out of the bedrooms first, I will pray over him about his asthma. I told the mother what I felt in my heart to do. She agreed.

Not long after that, guess who it was who came down from the bedrooms first? The very boy with the asthma! His mother and I asked if he would accept prayer for the asthmatic condition, and he agreed. We sat him down on a kitchen chair and laid hands on his shoulders as an extension of God's power to touch his body.

The three of us in the room were in agreement, so nobody in the room had unbelief in their hearts. The Scripture says in **Matthew 18:19, "Again I say to you that if two of you agree on** *earth concerning anything that they ask, it will be done for them by my Father in Heaven."*

While praying, I was aware that the Holy Spirit was bringing to my mind *John 10:10, "The thief does not come except to steal, kill and destroy. I* [Jesus] *have come that they may have life, and that they may have it more abundantly."*

With that Scripture in mind, I declared that the Lord rebuked the works of the thief over this boy's asthma, in Jesus' name.

That Scripture showed me this the attack of asthma was spiritual and nothing else. When the Holy Spirit reveals a Scripture like this at a time of prayer for someone, it cancels out all the pleading and crying and begging that can happen. The Holy Spirit gives us the Scripture, which brings revelation to the situation. We have the word of command in agreement with the Lord, which releases the power of the Lord to work. There was no need for us to do anything else, only to give thanks to the Lord in faith for His work over this boy's life.

We do not have to be scared about prayer because it is all about what the Holy Spirit is revealing to us. We simply need to come into agreement with Him and declare it.

Some time had passed before I asked this woman how her son was doing. She said that after we prayed he had not had an asthma attack.

It gave me great encouragement to see God's Word come to pass and set this boy free from his bondage. It gave me faith and courage to continue on that course.

It is all about listening to God in the circumstances of everyday life. I've learned to ask Him what is His purpose for me being with these people in this situation. Sometimes it is just to demonstrate God's love to people and serve them in any way we can, and a lot of the time it is like that.

I have a little note in my Bible from Jack Hayford on the Kingdom of God. He said:

> *The whole of Jesus' own preaching, teaching and ministry centred in these words;*

*"The kingdom of God is at hand" (Mark 1:15).
He came as the Saviour—a lamb to rescue and redeem
mankind to know his original estate in the divine order.
The dynamic of Christian life and ministry is found in
understanding "the kingdom of God, which is not in
eating and drinking (that is, ritual performance), but
in righteousness and peace and joy in the Holy Spirit"
(Romans 14:17).*[11]

Claire's Panic Attack After Childbirth

When our first two children, Matthew and Simon, were very
small, we had need of a child-minder because Geraldine was
working in the bank, and I was also working. We were fortunate
to find a lovely woman to mind our two boys. I will call her
Claire, which is not her real name, but I will use it for the sake
of the story. Over the course of time, we got to know Claire and
her family, and felt the liberty to share the gospel with her and her
family. Claire listened to what we had to say about the Lord as we
sowed God's Word into her heart. The only other thing we could
do was pray for her. It is God alone who causes His life to grow in
a person's life.

Later Claire became pregnant. Everything was fine through
the pregnancy, but when the day came to give birth to the baby,
something went wrong, which caused Claire to have a panic attack.
Geraldine and I were not aware of this until we went in to see
her and the baby the following day. Claire could not sleep, eat, or
receive any visitors, and was in a desperate state.

When we asked if we could see her for just two minutes, the
nurse would not guarantee that we could get in. We had already
sown the seed of God's Word in her heart many months before
this, and now Claire was in great need of help and ready to receive
prayer. The nurse returned from Claire's room and said you can
just go in for two minutes.

---

11 Notes from Spirit-Filled Life ® Bible.

We did just that. We said to Claire, "Would you like us to pray for you?"

Claire replied, "Yes."

Without further ado, we laid our hands on her forehead and invited the Holy Spirit to come and cover all her fears and anxieties. We declared to Claire that Jesus was the Prince of Peace over her and finished praying in the name of Jesus. We left her room, leaving her with the Holy Spirit.

The next day we went back to see Claire in the hospital to see what the Holy Spirit had done for her. We went there with expectation in our hearts, knowing that the Lord heard our prayers. When we walked down the corridor that led to her room, a woman who was jumping for joy and grinning from ear to ear. Yes, it was Claire!

She told us that as soon as we left the room, the Holy Spirit put her into a deep sleep for eighteen hours and she never felt better. The only person who got thanks for that was Jesus. He is our ever-present help in time of need, and He is the Prince of Peace.

I met Claire twenty-three years after this event, and she told me that in all that time she never had another panic attack. Praise God.

Chapter 5

Geraldine's Decision to Leave the Bank and Start a Bed & Breakfast Business

IT was at the time, when Geraldine was expecting our third child, that the pressure really mounted for us. Geraldine had to decide whether she could continue to work full-time in the bank with three children at home, of if she needed to discontinue her work with the bank.

Geraldine really wanted to rear her children herself, rather than farm them out to other people to rear. To take care of her own children would allow her full opportunity to impact their lives in a godly way. Therefore, she began the task of seeking the Lord's direction for this situation. She felt that a wise person makes their way sure. So how do we make our way sure?

Taking the principle from *Luke 14:28,* the Scripture instructs us: *"What man before building a house, does not first sit down and count the cost."* We were not building a house, but we were about to make a decision regarding our financial income that could either prosper or cripple us. We both looked at my income as a self-employed working man and I was not earning enough to keep every bill paid on my own. Geraldine was concerned that if she left the bank and stayed at home, she would not have enough money to put bread on the table. She feared that we would be at each other's throats and end up divorcing.

When making a decision like this, we cannot just "trust God" and be mindless about it. God has given us a mind to be able to think through it and be practical, but above all to ask the Lord to direct us. *Proverbs 16:3,* says, *"Commit your works to the Lord, and your thoughts will be established."* The Scriptures also say in *Psalm 127:1a, "Unless the Lord builds the house, they labour in vain who build it."*

That means it's necessary to have the Lord's leading and direction in these important matters, otherwise our labour or efforts could end up in vain. Labouring is hard enough at the best of times, but to labour in vain is worse. It also means that if we have the Lord's direction, we can be assured of His provision.

Geraldine found that with the pressures of work, plus family and church life, it was very difficult for her to have a prolonged time with the Lord—seeking His heart and direction. Nevertheless, it was imperative to find God's Word in this matter, so she went away for a whole day to a friend's house. She could be alone there all day, leaving her free of distractions to hear God's still, small voice.

The Holy Spirit led her to read through the Psalms, and when she got to *Psalm 37,* the Lord cancelled the fears and concerns she had in her heart and started to direct her.

Verse 4 says, *"Delight yourself also in the Lord, and He shall give you the desires of your heart."*

What were Geraldine's desires?

To leave the bank and rear her children at home.

Verse 5 says, *"Commit your way to the Lord, trust also in Him, and He shall bring it to pass."*

That was encouraging to her. She was in the process of doing it.

Verse 8 says, *"Do not fret—it only causes harm."*

Verse 23 says, *"The steps of a good man (woman) are ordered by the Lord, and He delights in his way."*

Verse 24 says, *"Though he fall, he shall not be utterly cast down for the Lord upholds him with His hand."*

Even if we made a mistake, God had all the doors covered, as it were. The Lord, through His Word, was giving Geraldine such encouragement to enable her to come to a place of making a decision.

Verse 25 capped it all for her. The Psalmist said this when he was an old man, having gone through life: *"I have been young, and now am old; yet I have not seen the righteous forsaken, nor His descendants begging bread."*

Indeed, God's Word cancelled *all* her fears.

She knew that she could leave the bank, but she still did not know what to do about income. She had to hear from God a bit more to know what to do because my income was still not enough.

When we still ourselves and refuse to get into a twist or a panic, then we are in a good place to hear God speak to us. We can see this in *1 Kings 19:12.* After Elijah won a great battle, he was so drained of emotional energy that when the woman Jezebel threatened him, he ran for his life and hid in a cave.

God did not speak to Elijah in the spectacular ways through the wind, earthquake or fire, but in *"...a still small voice."*

Sometime later Geraldine was reading *Isaiah 30:21.* God alerted her and she felt an urgency to take note of what it said: *"Your ears shall hear a word behind you, saying, "This is the way, walk in it, whenever you turn to the right hand or whenever you turn to the left."*

God was directing and preparing the way, to make her attentive to an idea that was yet to dawn on her. I call it a revelation. God had forewarned her so that it would not pass her by without apprehending it. It was important that she was on the alert.

Not long after this, she was on her morning coffee break with some other women in the Bank. For some reason they were talking among themselves about Bed & Breakfast as a job. They were discussing how you could be at home with your children, and depending on your location, you could have a steady income.

When Geraldine returned to her desk after the coffee break, a revelation came to her, just as she was about to sit down in her chair. "Bed & Breakfast" was the word in her ear that God had spoken to her. That was it! A Bed & Breakfast! She thought, "I could be at home with my children to rear them, and I could also have an income."

After that, whenever we asked anybody what he or she thought about a Bed & Breakfast as a means of income, every single person without exception said it was a good idea.

It can take time to hear the full word of direction from the Lord, and so if we are in a panic or inclined to be hasty, our actions may cause us harm. As in Psalm 37:8, we could end up doing the wrong thing or going the wrong way.

We now knew the way the Lord was directing us in, therefore, our next course of action was to try and sell our existing house and buy a new house. The location of our existing house was not in the right location or suitable for Bed & Breakfast purposes. It also wasn't large enough. I will describe our journey to you in another chapter of finding that house for Bed & Breakfast purposes.

In writing this, I am safe and secure as we submit our lives and everything pertaining to our lives into the hands of the Lord. We want to let the lord be Lord of our life, otherwise can we really say, *"Jesus is Lord?"*

We will always prosper in every way when we submit to Him.

God Showing Me There was a Girl in Geraldine's Womb

God was training me in how to discern His voice. When Geraldine discovered she was pregnant with our third child, she wondered about whether it was the right time for her to have another child.

We see in *Genesis 29:31* that the Lord opened Leah's womb. Also in *Genesis 30:22,* it states that God opened Rachel's womb. We see in *1 Samuel 1:5* that the Lord closed Hannah's womb for a time and for a purpose.

Knowing the Scriptures and that we are in the Lord's hands, we can stay calm. A Christian friend comforted Geraldine and encouraged her with *Psalm 84:11* which says, **"No good thing will He withhold from those who walk uprightly."** This pregnancy was in God's plan. With that sorted, we embraced what God had for us.

At that time in our lives, we held a Bible study and prayer group in our home. One night when Geraldine was many months into her pregnancy, she was not able to attend the prayer group meeting, but asked us to pray for her during the meeting. After I announced her request for prayer to the group, the Holy Spirit recalled to me a verse during the time of prayer in *Proverbs 18:22.* I wondered why I got it, because it did not seem to have any bearing on our prayers for her. Nevertheless, I delivered it to the group and it said, *"He who finds a wife finds a good thing, and obtains favour from the Lord."*

I recalled *Psalm 84:11,* which our friend quoted to encourage Geraldine about not withholding any "good thing."

I was reminded of *2 Corinthians 13:1,* where Paul states, *"This will be the third time I am coming to you. By the mouth of two or three witnesses every word shall be established."*

Here, I had as it were, two Scriptures, referring to the same situation. On the other hand, could I call them witnesses? The "good thing" referred to in *Psalm 84:11* on its own could mean anything. But when it was linked to *Proverbs 18:22,* he who finds a wife (female gender) finds a "good thing," that pinpointed the whole thing. I dared to declare to the group that there was a baby girl in Geraldine's womb. The group knew before Geraldine did!

Well, when the baby came I was not disappointed with my declaration of the gender by faith. The Lord gave us a beautiful baby girl, whom we named Elena, which means "the wise one; the bright one." She is now a young elegant woman whose heart is after the Lord.

Our Second Home

This little story illustrates how I was pressured to raise the offer I had already made on the house I was about to buy. The Lord gave me Scriptures to help me make my decisions and gave me victory in the end.

We had bought our first house just before we got married. We were there five years when the Lord directed us to go into the Bed & Breakfast industry. We had no firm offers on our own house but the real estate agent had guided us to the price we should expect. Our house was not in the right area for doing a Bed & Breakfast. My friend Tom put it to me this way, "If you want to preach the gospel you don't go to the desert, you go to where the people are."

With that in mind, we prayed about the location—where the tourists go and the price of the house was not outside our reach.

Sometime later, we found a house in Salthill, Galway. This house had been functioning as a Bed & Breakfast for many years. It had seven bedrooms. Our family was small in number at that time. The house fitted well with us, and we had a sense of God's peace about it. The price was within reach, and to our surprise, we felt we had room to combine family and business in the house. It was in the right location. Therefore, we told the Lord that we did not feel the need to look anywhere else, and so we made our offer.

Just after this, the real estate agent rang me one night at 9:30 p.m. and said he had a couple wanting to buy the house signed, sealed, and delivered that night. They had increased our offer by £2500 and he wanted to know where we stood. Thinking fast, I thought my God always shows up on the 11th hour. I told him I would let him know at 11 a.m. the following day.

As I was self-employed, I took the first part of the morning off to pray for God's guidance.

We were in a dilemma up to 11 a.m. We did not know what to do. We did not feel any directive from God. When 11 a.m. struck, I told Geraldine that I had a phone call to make and I did not know what to say.

I got up off the couch and walked to the phone when God spoke to me through the Scriptures. The first Scripture was *Luke 14:28, "For which of you, intending to build a tower [a house] does not sit down first and count the cost, whether he has enough to finish it."* The second Scripture came from *Psalm 37:8 "Do nothing in haste—it leads only to evildoing, do not fret—it only causes harm."*

I had a tablemat that read, "If you love something, set it free, if it comes back to you, it is yours. If it doesn't, it never was."

I knew what to do:

Since I had not sold my own house yet, starting a price war was unwise:

1. This real estate agent was pressuring me into a hasty situation.

2. I was learning the principle that when you love something, you sometimes have to let it go.

3. I instructed the real estate agent to go ahead and sell the house, and I let it go to the other buyer. He was shocked because he thought I was interested in it. The people selling the house were equally shocked that I had let it go so easily also.

By obeying God's directions, I showed Him that He was in control and that we were not covetous.

When I put the phone down, we were sad because we felt the house had been the Lord's provision. I went to work but came back for lunch to find Geraldine jumping for joy at our front door. She said the real estate agent had just called and told her that the people who were adamant about buying the house last night had disappeared off the scene. They did not want the house anymore. My suspicion was that they never existed in the first place.

We knew the house was ours. We sold our own house at the price the real estate agent had suggested, and bought the house in Salthill at the price we had originally offered, rather than at the price the other couple were supposed to have offered.

I really learned a lesson then about holding things loosely in my hands.

God Fills a Woman's Oil Tank

This story goes back to the early 90s, when we had very little money. Geraldine found herself praying on a weekly basis with two other women. It was in the autumn season when they got together to pray for things the Holy Spirit was laying on their hearts. They continued into the winter season, when one of the women said that she needed oil to heat her house but she had no money. Therefore, they started asking the Lord to bless her and send in the money to help this woman fill her oil tank. Three weeks went by, and still the woman did not get the money she needed. It began to dawn on Geraldine's heart that maybe the Lord wanted her to pay for the oil that this woman needed. The weather was getting colder, as well.

Geraldine came home and conveyed to me about what the Lord was impressing upon her heart. We both agreed to bless this woman, but we could only find £60. We rang the oil company and asked them if they would deliver £60 worth of oil to this woman's home, but they said the minimum delivery amount was £80. We had to tell them the story that we were not able to pay anymore. After hearing us, they agreed to deliver £60 worth of oil to this woman.

You cannot out-give God. A few months passed, and we came to the month of April. We ran a Bed & Breakfast business and our guests began to arrive in busloads during that month. We then found ourselves in a predicament and needed to fill our own oil tank, as we had none to heat the house for our guests. With the tours, we had to wait until the following month before we got our money. Adding to the pressure was the fact that we ran out of money to fill our own oil tank. However, just at the right time, the Lord laid it on somebody's heart to give us a gift of £250.

God rewards unselfish giving to those in need with boundless liberty. Remember, if God wants you to give something away, He only wants to give you something greater in return.

God Sobers Up a Man at My B&B Table

During our season of providing people with a bed and breakfast in our house, one particular man came for about three to four years in a row during February for the Galway car rally. However, the final year he came, he brought a friend with him. For the sake of identifying them I will call the regular guest John and his friend Jack. I asked these men one night what time they wanted their breakfast in the morning and they said 8:30 a.m. The next morning, I got out of bed to get the breakfast ready for them and found Jack coming in the front door. He had not seen his bed all night, so I wondered whether my getting up to prepare breakfast was in vain, but I got up anyway.

Well 8:30 a.m. came and the two men appeared at the breakfast table. I said to Jack, "You did not get much sleep last night, did you?"

He said, "No, I was up all night drinking whiskey."

I was horrified and told him that he had put himself in grave danger. I was very concerned for him and said, "Do you mind if I pray for you?" He did not refuse, so I laid my hand on his shoulder and called for the Holy Spirit to sober him and take him out of danger in Jesus' name.

Across the table, John was observing all this going on. I finished my prayer and I stepped back from him. John observed Jack's countenance and said, "You have sobered up."

Jack then said when I laid my hand on him and prayed, a buzz went right down his spine. He asked me, "Did I do wrong?"

I told him that ***Ephesians 5:18*** says, ***"And do not be drunk with wine, (or spirits) in which is dissipation; but be filled with the Spirit."***

I said that God is not a killjoy, and He gives instructions in the Scripture that if we will obey them, we will be free from trouble and destruction. I said, "God, in His love for you right now, took you out of danger."

The two men ate their breakfast, even though Jack had been drinking whiskey all night.

On their departure from our Bed & Breakfast premises, Jack shook my hand with thanksgiving, and I could sense he was waiting for another buzz to go down his spine. However, no buzz came, as it only came when the Holy Spirit was at work.

The Power of the Tongue

The following story I am about to tell brings to reality the truth of the following Scripture. ***Proverbs 18:21*** says, ***"Death and*** *life are in the power of the tongue, and those who love it will eat its fruit."*

Many years ago, I was called to a house to improve the storage area of a utility room and tile its floor. When that was finished, I was asked to tackle the kitchen—to take out the old units, put in new kitchen units, and tile its floor as well.

I started working in the utility room and within a very short space of time, I had completed the jobs there. I then progressed to the kitchen, where I took all the old units out and started to prepare for the new units. However, there was something different about this room because I began to encounter difficulties, obstacles, hindrances, and delays. This brought me to a place of praying and bringing it before the Lord because it was beyond the normal hiccups you get on a job. I asked the Lord to show me what I was fighting against because there was such a contrast between this room and the utility room.

Within a day or two after praying to the Lord, I was having a chat with the woman of the house during a coffee break. She made a very interesting comment and said, "Several tradesmen came here to measure up the job to give me a price for the new kitchen, but none of those tradesmen ever came back to me about the job.

Because of this, I began to say, "This kitchen will *never* be done."

Prior to this conversation, I had knowledge of the above Scripture in the Book of Proverbs. I heard her say those words, and the Lord gave me discernment about the obstacles and hindrances relating to the job.

I was fighting against the power of her words, but because the woman did not have the knowledge of the Scripture, she was unaware of the power of the words she had spoken and their negative consequences.

I advised her to repent of the words she had spoken over the kitchen, meaning to turn away from saying them again, and I then broke the power of those words in Jesus' name.

My discernment was correct because I had no sooner broken the power of those words than the work on the kitchen began to flow beautifully. The kitchen got finished and the whole family was very pleased with the job. Moreover, we have been the best of friends ever since.

Chapter 6

The Disaster of a Trip to France and of God Restoring a Trip to Majorca

*P*ROVERBS 18:21 *says, "Death and life are in the power of the tongue, and those who love it will eat its fruit."*

What we speak is extremely important! We can bless and curse others and ourselves with the same tongue. We can verbalise a vow out of a traumatic situation and find ourselves imprisoned because of the words spoken. The best thing, of course, is to get a hold of God's promises in the Bible, and then to absorb them into our lives and be transformed in our thinking by His Word! We will begin to learn what to say, and what not to say. If we live and speak according to His Word, we will find ourselves in a very safe place.

Romans 12:2 says, *"And do not be conformed to this world, but be transformed by the renewing of your mind, That you may prove what is that good and acceptable and perfect will of God."*

Geraldine and I always struggled with the cash flow. We constantly stretched ourselves in the walk of faith concerning our material expansion, and we were strapped for cash a lot of the time. We both worked hard and our family was increasing, therefore there were constant demands on our resources. I found myself saying many times, "We have no money." However, one day the Holy Spirit convicted me of the words I was speaking. This was not a condemning word—as if I was a criminal—but rather a check on my spirit or a convincing in my heart that my words expressing the reality of the situation were, in fact, wrong. I needed to stop saying those specific words, "We have no money!"

I knew then what I had to do. I repented to the Lord of those words, and instead I just told my heavenly Father the dilemma I was in. Then I would wait and see what He would say to me. It is always good for us to be reliant on the Lord and dependent upon Him.

A Scripture that is well worth taking note of in relation to riches or the lack of it is in **Proverbs 30:7-9:**

> **Two things I request of you** [Deprive me not before I die]**: Remove falsehood and lies far from me; give me neither poverty nor riches—feed me with the food allotted to me; lest I be full and deny you, and say, "Who is the Lord?" or lest I be poor and steal, and profane the name of my God.**

Another verse is **Philippians 4:19**, which states, **"And my God shall supply all your need according to His riches in glory by Christ Jesus."**

We need to be very careful when applying this verse to our situations. We have to look at the context in which it was written. These people at Philippi were generous with their giving to the Apostle Paul in the work of his ministry, and as a response to their giving, he spoke this verse to them.

Both Geraldine and I examined ourselves in the matter of giving and we found ourselves to be all right, so we felt we could apply this verse to our situation.

The Word of God is our plumb line and gives us direction. When we come into the knowledge of it, we receive it by faith and put it into action.

1. In God's ordinary means of operating, people do not come to saving faith unless they either read the Bible or have someone tell them the gospel message that is in it. It is the Word of God that the Holy Spirit uses to awaken a response of faith within us. Moreover, it is the reliability of the Word of God on which we rest our faith for salvation. The Scriptures are the words of eternal life. **(See James 1:18; 1 Peter 1:23).** This is why preaching the gospel is absolutely necessary **(See Hebrews 10).**[12]

---

12 Ibid.

2. How do we please God? *Hebrews 11:6.* (See Chapter 2).

Here is another Scripture: ***Deuteronomy 8:18, "And you shall remember the Lord your God, for it is He who gives you the power*** [or ability] ***to get wealth."***

Here comes the story.

Our big need at this time was a family holiday. We had four children and we ran a Bed & Breakfast business. But as I said earlier, we were short of the cash needed for the holiday. It was in the autumn of 1997 when I repented to the Lord of my negative confession and began to say instead, "Lord, you supply all our needs and in this instance we need a holiday, badly. I do not expect money to be pushed through the letterbox, but give us the ability to get the money needed to go on a family holiday in the spring of 1998."

We sat down together and worked out the cost of the whole holiday so that we knew what we needed to ask the Lord. That gave us a clear focus. With the children being so young, it had to be a camping trip, so we focused on a trip to southern France with euro camp.

We had six months to gather the money, so we broke it down to manageable sizes and estimated the amount we would have to save each month. We diligently put the money aside, and by God's grace, we actually *had* that amount each month! When the money for the deposit was required, we had it. We put down the deposit, so now we were committed to it. Come April 1998, we were on our way. We brought our car with us via the ferry and proceeded south. Our car was a Citroën at that time, which is significant to the story.

We were about two days into our holiday, driving happily around the countryside and enjoying the breath taking views. We drove over a roughly laid railway track, when suddenly without any warning, something heavy fell from our car onto the roadway. After investigation, we saw that our gearbox had fallen out onto the road. Stranded on the spot, we had no clue as to where we were. Neither did we know where the nearest garage was. We had little knowledge of the French language either, as Geraldine knew only a few words.

It was a Saturday, so we did not know if any garages were open. After being on the side of the road for what seemed like an eternity, somebody finally stopped who had knowledge of the place and knew a bit of English. They got us to a garage that was open. The process of getting the mechanic to our car and towing it back to his garage took another couple of hours.

With a Citroën, we were in the right country to get it repaired as they manufacture them there. It was very hard to get a mechanic to work on a Citroën back in Galway, as they were too complicated to work on. Luckily, we had taken out insurance with respect to this holiday. We had to ring a car hire depot and got another car to keep us mobile. The mechanic informed us that it could take four to five days to repair the car.

The next thing we heard was that something had happened back home, and we decided that Geraldine must return to Ireland. She decided to take a flight the next day, which was a Monday. I cannot remember where we got the money. Maybe we used plastic!

It was with two heavy hearts on that Sunday afternoon, with the two of us crying out to God. I thought, "The devil has robbed us of a holiday that the Lord has enabled us to have and we received by faith." I said that to Geraldine there and then.

Scripture says that God is a restorer. After I spoke out my thoughts, Geraldine told me that before I spoke she had been thinking the same thing. I said, "Since the two of us are thinking the same thing at the same time, let's pray to the Father." We were both aware of a scriptural promise in *Matthew 18:19* which states, *"Again I say to you that if two of you agree on earth concerning anything that they ask, it will be done for them by my Father in heaven."*

With the knowledge of this Scripture and the procedure we had taken for this holiday, we were sure that God was going to agree with whatever we asked of Him. In prayer, in the car, we came before our heavenly Father to give Him thanks for this holiday and

His provision. We said, "Father, we have been robbed by the devil of this holiday. We are asking you to restore to both of us a holiday that will not cost us anything."

We both agreed, and left it in the Lord's hands. We proceeded with getting Geraldine to the airport for her trip the next day. I continued with the holiday on the campsite with our four young children. Eventually, after a few days, we got our own car back and our holiday period ended. When the children's ages are between four and eleven, all they need are a few simple things—a pool, a playground and a sand pit with a lot of food. Very simple stuff, really!

Our journey home began, and we had to drive two-thirds of the length of France. This was my second time driving through France. Everything was quite new and Matthew, my co-driver, was nearly eleven years old. He did an absolutely wonderful job paying sterling attention to the road signs all along the way. That was a big task for a young man of his age!

When we were near Paris, I stopped off at a petrol station. We purchased some bags of sweets for the children and not long after that, all that muck came spewing out of the mouth of my four-year-old, who was in the middle of the back seat. As a result, my left arm and the hand break were covered in it. You could imagine me singing, "Oh Holy God, the stars are shining brightly!" No! I do not think you could. More like "Shine on Harvest Moon." Anyway, we finally got home in one piece and Geraldine was fine.

The months of May, June, July, and August passed by, and nothing seemed to happen about the holiday that we had lost and asked in prayer to be restored. Then, the children returned to school in the first week of September. They came home with raffle tickets where the proceeds would go towards a building fund. It caught my eye that the first prize was worth a £500 holiday to the Isle of Man. I wondered if this was the Lord's provision of that holiday for which we had asked. I took a few books of raffle tickets home to purchase. Then the next thing was I could not find them anywhere. Every time I went down to the school, I had it in my mind to get another few books to purchase. I was thinking, "if you are not in you cannot win." But, every time I went to the school, I forgot to get more tickets. Before I knew it, the day of the raffle had come and gone, so I missed that chance, or so I thought.

Sometime later Geraldine called over to our neighbours—who actually attended the same church gathering as we did—to have a chat. While having a cup of coffee, the woman of this house handed a large envelope to Geraldine and said something like, "We have enough of these things anyway, so you take this."

Geraldine did not understand what the woman was talking about until she opened the envelope. She discovered that our Christian neighbour had won the raffle for the £500 trip to the Isle of Man and had given it to us! God surely works in mysterious ways. He is such a faithful God!

Following our return home from France that April, I had tried to get money back from the holiday insurance, but to no avail. I was due about £130. I knew the travel agent who had put up the prize of the holiday to the Isle of Man, so I asked him if we were restricted to the Isle of Man or could we choose anywhere else. He said, "No bother." However, he said that if our other choice of destination needed more money, we would have to pay the difference. In the meantime, we looked for a deal on the Island of Majorca, as it is still lovely and warm at the end of September and early October, and all the hotels are still open.

We eventually found a deal for a full board with flights included for two at a cost of £600. God's provision is always on time. We finally got the £130 insurance refund we had been looking for all summer, just in time to pay for our holiday to Majorca, and had £30 extra to spend. The Lord is so faithful. This is not about a formula. It is about applying scriptural principles to our lives and being in relationship with the Father.

I hope you have been encouraged.

Chapter 7

Geraldine Leading a Woman to Christ

HERE was a woman whom Geraldine knew very well, and she had often shared with her about her relationship with the Lord and all the things pertaining to God.

One time this woman got very ill and had to go to hospital. Geraldine visited her quite often and was very concerned for her salvation. Every time Geraldine's visit ended, she would ask her if she would like to pray. The woman agreed, so they would say together the Lord's Prayer. After praying, Geraldine would continue with her own prayer—whatever words that the Lord might impress upon her heart.

One night while they were together not saying anything about prayer or the Lord, the woman burst out with an objection to this "born again" stuff, saying, "The prayers you say mean nothing to me."

Now I need to point out that we humans here on Earth are visible to each other, but we must never ignore the fact that there is a spiritual world. It's invisible to our naked eyes, but just as real and infinitely more powerful than anything visible. We cannot see the wind, but we can see the effects of it.

On the one hand, we have Father God, Jesus, and the Holy Spirit, along with their ministering angels who love us more than we could ever imagine. Father God, who made us in His own image and likeness, wants us to be saved. He wants us to be with Him for eternity through putting our trust in Jesus Christ and His death on the Cross. Father requires us to come into relationship with Him through Jesus. In other words, for us to know Him and Him to know us, we secure our eternal life as opposed to eternal death or separation. Moreover, He enables us to know Him through His Word by the Holy Spirit. All this is pivotal for our acceptance from Father. Therefore, God, by His Spirit, the Scriptures and His ministering angels, tries to influence us.

They are not alone in the spiritual world, however. There is also Satan, also called Lucifer. He was the worship leader in Heaven, but when pride entered into him, he thought that he should be on the throne of God. He was then thrown out of Heaven and flung down to Earth. In his rebellion, he influenced a third of the angels and they were also thrown out of Heaven and were cast down to Earth. Hence, Satan is called "the god of this world." His jurisdiction is here and we are in the middle of it all. Satan and his minions, who hate us, are doing their utmost to destroy, steal, and kill us. He wants to keep us ignorant and fearful of the knowledge and the glory of God. I say all this as a backdrop to what I am about to tell you.

So now we get back to the story. After this woman's comment, there was little further conversation that evening. Geraldine drove home very despondent with her head hanging low, when all of a sudden the Holy Spirit reminded her that there were two powers at work. Because she knew the Scriptures and was filled with the Holy Spirit, He gave her power to rise above the onslaught of the enemy, who was trying to destroy and steal, and so she raised her head again. The Scripture in *1 John 4:4* states, ***"You are of God, little children, and have overcome them, because He*** [Jesus] ***who is in you is greater than he*** [the devil] ***who is in the world."***

A few days later, Geraldine returned to visit her friend and when her meeting had ended, the Holy Spirit once again gave Geraldine strength and courage. She suggested to her the possibility of finishing the evening with the Lord's Prayer.

She agreed and when the Lord's Prayer was finished, she said to Geraldine, "And your own prayers?"

Geraldine did so, and asked her if she wanted to invite the Lord Jesus into her heart and put her trust in His finished work on the Cross. She said yes!

Geraldine could hardly believe her ears, especially after what the woman said the previous evening. That previous evening's comment had been like the last roar of the enemy, discouraging both women. First, by attempting to make Geraldine give up on this woman, and aiming to prevent her doing the work God had ordained for her to do. Second, her friend was also under attack with suggestions by "the enemy" via other people suggesting that she reject Jesus and anything to do with "being born again."

However, God got the victory through prayer, the power of the Holy Spirit, and Geraldine's obedience in drawing this woman to Him with her confession of faith. *Romans 10:9* states, *"That if you confess with your mouth the Lord Jesus and believe in your heart that God raised Him from the dead, you shall be saved."*

Not long after that night, this precious woman died, but her spirit went to be present with the Lord forever. As it says in *2 Corinthians 5:8, "We are confident, yes, well pleased rather to be absent from the body and to be present with the Lord."*

Let me illustrate through Scripture that if anyone of us, even on our deathbed—the 11th hour, 59 minutes of our life—accept Jesus Christ into our hearts as our Saviour, we will be saved. As illustrated in the parable in the workers in the vineyard in *Matthew 20:1-16,* we will receive the same wages as those who were called to labour in the vineyard at the break of day. *Verses 9-10* say, *"And when those came who were hired about the eleventh hour, they each received a denarius. But when the first came, they supposed they would receive more; and they likewise received each a denarius."*

In *John 3,* Jesus was talking to Nicodemus, who was thoroughly trained in Jewish law and theology. Nicodemus recognised Jesus as a teacher come from God. In *verse 3,* Jesus answered and said to him, *"Most assuredly, I say to you, unless one is born again, he cannot see the kingdom of God."* The Greek word translated "again" can also be rendered, "from above." Nicodemus clearly understood it in the former sense, whereas Jesus had both meanings in mind. To enter the Kingdom of God, one must be born again, not by experiencing a second biological birth, but by spiritual birth from above.[13]

---

13 Ibid.

It just goes to show us the battle we are in, and the devil tries to stop us from coming to the knowledge of and trust in Jesus Christ and His saving grace. When somebody yields to Christ and His rule, it means that the power the devil had over that person previously has come to an end and he does not like it one bit because the tables are now turned on him. I encourage everyone to grow in the knowledge of God's Word. It is the means by which we fight the enemy. *Ephesians 6:17* says, *"And take the helmet of salvation, and the sword of the Spirit, which is the word of God;"*

There are some interesting verses in *Matthew 16:13-17, 21-23,* which indicate to us the influences we may come under either from God or the devil:

> *Verse 13: "When Jesus came into the region of Caesarea Philippi, He asked His disciples, saying, 'Who do men say that I, the Son of Man, am?'*
>
> *Verse 14: so they said, some say John the Baptist, some Elijah, and others Jeremiah or one of the prophets.*
>
> *Verse 15: He said to them, "But who do you say that I am?*
>
> *Verse 16: Simon Peter answered and said, 'You are the Christ, the Son of the living God,'*
>
> *Verse 17: Jesus answered and said to him, 'Blessed are you, Simon Bar—Jonah, for flesh and blood has not revealed this to you, but My Father who is in heaven.'*

Then within a very short space of time, only three verses, Jesus told them a few more things:

> *Verse 21: From that time Jesus began to show His disciples that He must go to Jerusalem, and suffer many things from the elders and chief priests and scribes, and be killed, and be raised the third day.*
>
> *Verse 22: Then Peter took Him aside and began to rebuke Him, saying, 'Far be it from you, Lord; this shall not happen to you!'*

Verse 23: but He turned and said to Peter, 'Get behind Me, Satan! You are an offense to Me, for you are not mindful of the things of God, but the things of men.'"

We could ask ourselves after hearing that comment from Jesus to Peter—was the Apostle Peter the pillar of the Church, or was it Satan? *Certainly not!* It was Jesus who recognised in Peter's *words* the same diabolically inspired temptation to avoid suffering as part of His messianic vocation, as He had heard in the wilderness. We will find it in **Matthew 4:10** where He spoke to Satan who was tempting Him. *"Away with you, Satan! For it is written, 'You shall worship the Lord your God, and Him only you shall serve.'"*[14]

If we do not have knowledge of the Scriptures with the Holy Spirit revealing to us the truths and His plan of salvation, how can we recognise the enemy working in our lives? We could, either Christian or non-Christian, be saying things such as the Apostle Peter said when he was not mindful of the things of God and ignorant of the plan of salvation.

An example of hearing from two different spiritual sources is Peter's statement in *Matthew 16:13-17, 21-23.* Father God himself inspired one statement, and very shortly after that, Peter was inspired by Satan to deter Jesus from doing the very thing Father God had commissioned Him to do. Peter did not want Jesus to die for selfish reasons.

We can be very sure of one thing—the moment any of us begins to follow the Lord and live for Him, or step out in faith in obedience to the command of God given from Scripture—that is the very moment the devil is going to show up. His aim is to deter us from obeying the Lord. On the other hand, if we are not doing any of these things, the devil will leave us alone because we pose no threat to him whatsoever. We are just living our lives the way he wants us to.

To encourage us, I have one verse of scriptural promise, which

---

14 Ibid.

comes from *James 4:7, "Therefore submit to God, Resist the devil and he will flee from you.* However, in *verse 6* we are warned that *"God resists the proud, but gives grace to the humble."*

There are some enlightening verses in *Ephesians 6:11-17* that will help us realise the forces that are against us, and instruct us on how to protect ourselves:

Verse 11: "Put on the whole armour of God that you may be able to stand against the wiles of the devil.

Verse 12: for we do not wrestle against flesh and blood, but against principalities, against powers, against the rulers of the darkness of this age, against spiritual hosts of wickedness in the heavenly places.

Verse 13: Therefore take up the whole armour of God, that you may be able to withstand in the evil day, and having done all, to stand.

Verse 14: Stand therefore, having girded your waist with truth, having put on the breastplate of righteousness,

Verse 15: and having shod your feet with the preparation of the gospel of peace;

Verse 16: above all, taking the shield of faith with which you will be able to quench all the fiery darts of the wicked one.

Verse 17: and take the helmet of salvation, and the sword of the Spirit, which is the word of God."

Every Christian in their walk of obedience to the Lord will be sure to engage the opposition and spiritual resistance of Satan and his minions. Hence, we have to be Spirit-filled warriors to face the enemy of our souls. We must continually "be strong" or strengthen ourselves with the armour provided as specified in the above verses. The ground of the warrior's strength is their position "in the Lord." Our strength is "the power of His might." When we, as spirit-filled Christians, take into account our position in Christ and appropriate the provided armour, the Holy Spirit empowers us to conquer this new life in resisting Satanic attack.

These Scriptures for many of us may send shivers up our spine, but we have nothing to fear as He has instructed us how to protect ourselves. The Lord, by the Holy Spirit, who lives in the surrendered soul, is greater than he [Satan] who lives in the world. Keep obeying the Lord. His yoke is easy and His burden is light. God is love and perfect love casts out fear. The Lord, by His Holy Spirit, living within us, enables us to live victoriously in this life.

Chapter 8

God Speaking to Geraldine Before Her Discovery of Cancer and her Life Through to Her Death

May I share a word that Jesus gave us in *John 16:33? "In me you may have peace. In the world you will have tribulation; but be of good cheer, I have overcome the world."*

If we are in Christ, meaning, trusting in His shed blood on the Cross for us, then He has given us authority in His name. Since He has overcome the world, He has given us the power to overcome the troubles that come upon us in this world. The following story is a testimony to the truth of this Scripture.

In January 1999, when Geraldine was studying the Bible, she happened to be reading *Joel 1,* and her eyes rested on *verse 4* which says, *"What the chewing locust left, the swarming locust has eaten; what the swarming locust left, the crawling locust has eaten; and what the crawling locust left, the consuming locust has eaten."*

She knew that the Lord had spoken to her, as those words were impressed upon her heart as she read them. She was sensing that there was great devastation on the way but did not know what form it was going to take. In addition to this Scripture, she felt the Lord telling her, **"Hold on to My Word"** and she wanted to say this ten times. In addition to this, she felt the Lord telling her, **"Wrap my Words around your heart even if it means a matter of life or death."**

Geraldine knew God had spoken to her, but she did not fully understand if this word was for her personally. She spoke it out to the church assembly in case somebody was in need of it, however, it did not rest on anybody.

One week later Geraldine found a lump in her breast and, upon examination, the doctors informed her that she had cancer. The Lord in His love for her had forewarned her of the tribulation that lay ahead through the word He had given her.

I remember when the doctor and nurses told us that she had cancer—we were both unaffected by it. It was as though the Lord had put a shield around us. They were looking for the look of horror and fear in our faces, but they found none.

Geraldine had to have a lumpectomy and radiotherapy, and had to take a certain medication for five years, but then had to stop taking it after that. This she did but six months later in August 2004, we found the cancer spreading to her sternum bone. This meant more treatment. The death threat was still with us. For the next four and a half years, the cancer continued to show up in other sites in her body. During this latter four and a half years, we sold our old house in March 2004 and rented another house while the two of us designed our new home.

I was a draughtsman and was able to draw up the plans of the new house. We were like two little pigs in muck—we were so happy. With our planning permission achieved, we broke ground on the plot of our new home in March 2005. April 2005 saw the foundations set, and in November 2005, we moved into it, but had no internal doors hung for another three months. The all-important door, of course, was the toilet door.

Moving into this house was a dream come true for us. Ever since we had married, nineteen years prior to this, it had been our dream to build our own home. All this progressive activity was happening when the cancer was becoming ever more invasive in her body. Nevertheless, there was no stopping Geraldine! Moreover, she did not lie down under the death threat that was cancer.

All these years, Geraldine had obeyed the Lord in all His leadings after she had found that lump. She held on to His Word and wrapped it around her heart. When negative thoughts came upon her to drag her down to despair, she drew close to the Lord and He never failed to comfort her. In the midst of this "death threat," she experienced the Kingdom of God: *"…righteousness, peace and joy in the Holy Spirit." (Romans 14:17).* When she had it, I had it, our children had it, and our dog had it. Nobody "lost their head" with frustration. The Lord enabled her to live in victory in the midst of this disease.

In May 2008, we discovered that calcium was leaking from her bones. This was really the beginning of the end for her, and it all got progressively worse from then on. At first, she was able to come home from hospital for a few days at a time following treatment, but it was not long before the doctors told her that she could not go home. She needed continuous treatment.

Come July and feeling trapped in hospital, Geraldine desperately wanted to get home—she thought she would never see it again.

On Thursday, 26th July 2008, Geraldine could not take any more treatment. The doctors could do no more for her. We prayed together and asked the Lord to raise her up out of this disease, and if He did not, to please take her home quickly. We did not know that within ten days she would be dead.

On Saturday, 24th July, with great difficulty, I got the hospital to agree to let her home. It took the weekend to arrange everything for a homecoming, and on Monday, 28th July, Geraldine arrived home to us with hospice care. It was an exhilarating moment for us to get her home, but a very sad moment because we knew that if there was not a miracle, she was going to die very soon.

My daughter Elena, who had gone on a holiday abroad two weeks prior to this development when everything seemed to be all right, returned home late on Thursday, the 31st July. Geraldine was awake and was able to greet her, but come Friday morning she did not open her eyes ever again. Just before noon on Saturday, 2nd August 2008, Geraldine died thirty seconds after her pastor Stephen Kenny had completed reading Psalms 1, Psalm 23 and Psalm 25. My precious champion, as I described her, had died in her tenth year of battling cancer. The Lord took her home.

The way Geraldine had conducted her life in the midst of this cancerous death threat was not alone an inspiration to me, but was an inspiration to my children, her own family, and to everyone who knew her. You would visit her in the hospital, but you would come away uplifted by her attitude, and even prayed for by her. You came away inspired. To this day, many people will witness to this fact.

I remember a particular day, about two weeks before she died. I came in to visit her in hospital. Her sister was already there with her. I listened to her and said, "You look and sound a bit stronger today, Ger."

She turned over to her sister and said, "Maybe we will get up the River Shannon on that cruise yet!" So many plans she had in her heart to do. She never gave up.

After she died, I could not help thinking of what the Lord had spoken to her about. Can you imagine the chewing, swarming, crawling, and consuming locusts? That is what it was like with the cancer. It went through her body and finally consumed her, and then she said that the Lord had said to her, "Hold on to My Word." Her comment straight after that was, "And I feel like saying it ten times." I think that these words are very interesting.

Daniel 7:25 talks about an event that is going to happen in the future and says, *"... For a time and times and half a time."* This is another way of saying, three and one-half years. Therefore, when Geraldine was saying the words, "And I feel like saying it ten times," it was as if the Lord was indicating to her and both of us that this was going to be a ten-year battle, and it was. However, at the time we did not know which way it was going to go. I think He did indicate to us that detail, but we did not comprehend it at the time, and I am glad we did not.

There is one fact that is true for us all, and that is we are going to die. We just do not know when or how. Many, many people fear cancer and even death, but if you have yielded your life to the lordship of Jesus and trust Him with your life here on Earth, when your spirit leaves your body after death, He is faithful to carry you through.

Chapter 9

Deep Hurt, Making Bad Vows, and the Aftereffects

TO begin the story, it is necessary for me to go right back to when my dad was a young teenager. He came from the midlands to work in Galway when he was fifteen years old. The company he came to work in had many departments in it—a grocery and provisions section, a public bar, tea blenders, and more.

While he was being apprenticed to the business, he did further studies, and as a result, he became the manager of the company at the age of twenty-nine. That was in 1933.

He was a faithful and righteous man, who had a heart for God. In 1968, after giving forty-nine years of faithful service to that one company, he was told that there was no place there for him anymore. The new directors had new plans for the company and he was not going to be a part of them.

With respect to a pension scheme, nothing had been put in place for him. From my limited understanding at the time, when he was let go he received neither thanks nor any financial remuneration for a lifetime of faithful service. He was just a discard!

What you or I perceive or understand of an event is how that event affects us, even if the facts about the situation are not fully correct. What I perceived about them at the time is what affected me so very negatively over the following years. This is what I hope to unfold to you.

I remember that when this happened, I never heard him say anything bad about anybody concerned, but in truth, he must have been hurt very deeply. By 1970—two years later—he was dead. My mother was left without a husband and his five children, ranging in age from thirteen to twenty, were left without their father.

I was profoundly affected by these events, and as a consequence, I made a vow that I would never be an employee. If this was the way employees got rewarded for giving lifelong faithful service, I wanted none of that.

This was a very bad and negative reaction. Nevertheless, this is what happens to those who experience trauma and injustice. We can go on and say things that can indeed imprison us for a very long time if we do not deal with the hurt. For the next thirty years, whenever I spoke about the loss of my dad and thought of what had happened to him, I broke down in tears.

In 1970, I suffered the loss of my earthly dad. Thirteen years later in 1983, I gained and found an everlasting heavenly Father through Jesus Christ.

Following my father's death, I spent eight years studying and six years working in companies under bosses between periods of study. When I was made redundant in 1984, the beginning of my self-employment period had arrived. I was my own boss now. The vow of never wanting to be an employee was coming to pass.

For the next fifteen years I was chipping away at my self-employed carpentry and maintenance work. God himself was doing His "chipping away" at *my* old block. He was showing me other areas of my life that needed alteration in order to give glory to His name. However, the day of reckoning came for me. He brought to my attention, in the powerful way that He does, that my attitude towards authority was out of order. The Holy Spirit wanted to bring more freedom into my life.

My heart wanted to please my heavenly Father and to become like the character of Christ. I gladly repented to Him to become right. The question was why was I like this? I had to get to the root cause of it so that it would not reappear again. Within a couple of minutes, the Holy Spirit brought me back to its root cause. He showed me the vow I made of not wanting to work as an employee after my dad was so badly treated. I had struggled with authority all those years because I never conquered my emotional memories in connection with my dad's incident.

Now that this came to light, I was in a place to do something about it, and I did just that. I had some repenting and forgiveness to deal with, also I needed to cut off the power of the vow. I broke it in Jesus' name and asked the Holy Spirit to cleanse me and heal my emotional memories. This does not happen overnight, but I was now on a much better road.

Within a very short time of dealing with this old problem, I took time out from my self-employment business in January 2002 and became an employee in a company loading vending machines. I loved and respected my new boss, but three and a half years into that job I had to leave that employment. I had to supervise on a full-time basis the building of my new house, which Geraldine and I designed together. I was the contractor and building it by direct labour.

After my repentance, God changed and healed my heart and within a very short time, He opened the door of opportunity for me to put my new heart and attitude into practice. He wanted me to experience His work of healing in me and test it out. I discovered that I did fine. He brought all that about just in time and before I was swallowed up in the activity of building my own house. After my house was built, life brought me in another direction. As Scripture says, *"He makes all things beautiful in their time."*

Jesus loves us the way we are at any given moment, but He loves us too much to leave us where we are! We need to mature, get rid of the baggage that weighs us down, and be healed and delivered of the hurts, damages, and bad vows that have affected and imprisoned us.

Remember, we have the power of the Holy Spirit at our disposal to help us. Therefore, we must entrust ourselves to Him to empower us to get free and liberated. Jesus is the gateway to freedom and He will bring it to pass if we are committed to Him and His purposes.

My Struggle to Come Down off the Podium

My sporting and music life during my formative years had a major impact in my life. Some of the offshoots of what I achieved in these areas were competing or struggling to manifest in later years while living as a Spirit-filled Christian.

As a teenager and a young man in my early twenties, I was a local and provincial swimming champion, forever on the podium receiving gold medals for my achievements. I was on the provincial schoolboy rugby team. I coached swimming and later on coached senior school rugby teams. I captained my school rugby team for a season. I was also a very talented singer and musician with good looks thrown in. I played the guitar and performed in the pubs and some cabaret acts. I performed on stage and sang in musicals.

I was always on the podium, in the limelight receiving applause and acclaim from admirers. Even though I had all these talents and gifts, I struggled greatly with insecurity. A lack of confidence lurked constantly in the background.

I hope to convey to you the battle I had when I became a born-again Christian. I had said goodbye to, or as Scripture puts it, I had put to death my old life, my old nature as it were. As the Apostle Paul puts it, *"It is no longer I who live, but Christ who lives in me."*

I was put to the test especially when I started attending a Christian church assembly. I was put in the place of leading the worship ministry because some of the students who had been leading it had come to the end of their college studies and were leaving town to find work. I did the best I could in my raw state of Christianity, but here I was again on stage and in the limelight. I was trying to put to death the old self that was screaming to stay alive. However, I was in the best place for God to highlight that hidden desire of achievement and acclaim that wanted to rise up in me so He could expose it.

What a struggle I had to come down off that podium in my heart! My need to be in the limelight—to be on stage with the need for recognition—was like a drug most of the time because I have been in that highlighted position for so long. I was unaware of that need, for the most part. Nevertheless, I used to get a check in my spirit on occasion. My heart was now trying to please Jesus and give Him glory.

The Lord had captured me and even better, He had rescued and saved me from myself in the process, as well as from eternal damnation. I became a work in progress, and may I say I am still a work in progress. However, I have come a long way in the reconstruction process.

Even though Scripture declares that we are dead to self, the putting to death of our self-centred life is a process. Some areas can take many years to demolish, and then you must take on the task of building the Christ-centred life in its place. This is very strong language. In other words, getting to the place where the old man, the old sinful nature, is no longer having total rule over our lives can be a long slow process. But we can get there because when we are in Christ, we have the power to change. I hope that is clear. The process of transformation into the image of Christ takes time as the Word of God and the Holy Spirit working in our life renews us in our mind. When people look at me now and observe my life, I hope that they see the character of Christ shining through me, rather than seeing the old self-centred, self-conscious, ugly me. All we need to do is surrender to Jesus Christ and He does the rest in causing us to grow more like Him.

After walking with the Lord for twenty-eight years, I have no more cravings to be in the spotlight as I once had. My identity is firmly rooted in Christ and not in my singing, playing guitar, or any other physical achievement. I am secure in Him and I do not need the props any longer. I have stopped striving after any positions. I am content with who I am in Christ and I am calm now, and I can tell you it is so liberating.

I just love asking the Lord to give me opportunities to come alongside people and share my faith or encourage them in Christ. The writing of this book is a privilege for me and I hope a great benefit to you in seeing how I have conducted my life under the authority of God's Word these last twenty-eight years.

Chapter 10

Speaking to a Van Engine in Trouble

FOR a period of three and a half years during my working life, I took a break from carpentry and painting and worked for a vending machine company. I had a van that was full of sweets and drinks and went around filling their machines with these. My children thought Heaven had come to Earth. My boss loved to hear this. The van had an engine that was always spluttering and stopping on me. This made my job very difficult. If it malfunctioned on a remote part of the road where help would be difficult to get, it put me under a lot of pressure to try to get all my calls accomplished within the already full day.

This malfunction happened quite a bit in the first few months of my new job. We tried without success to get it fixed. One day I was driving back to the depot and as I was approaching the town, the van started to splutter on me again. I tried to keep driving because I knew I was approaching the mechanic the company used to fix their vans.

When I arrived at the mechanic's garage—you guessed right— the van's engine was working perfectly. I got so frustrated with this engine, and I was at the end of my tether with it. I spoke out to the engine and commanded it to perform the way it had been performing in secret on the road. I commanded this engine to stop hiding the malfunction and come public, in Jesus' name. The mechanic was listening to all of this.

I am sure this mechanic never in his life heard anybody talk to an engine. I am sure he was thinking that there was a place for me, and it was not in the public domain, but I did not mind. I knew that with man it is impossible, but with God all things are possible, and everything in Heaven and Earth is under the authority of Jesus.

Therefore, for me to speak to this engine as instructed in Scripture was a demonstration of my faith in Jesus. After all, Jesus spoke to demons to come out of a man. Jesus spoke to Lazarus—who was dead—and commanded him to rise up. Jesus spoke to a tree—He cursed it and it withered. This is what a "kingdom life" looks like. Jesus is always my model for how to live.

After speaking to this engine, I had to wait for about one minute, knowing that this mechanic was thinking that I was for the birds. Finally, after what seemed like a lifetime of waiting, that old engine came out of hiding. It started to splutter as it had in private. Jesus had rescued me. The mechanic was amazed and asked me if I always spoke like that.

I replied, "Only when necessary." He had never seen or heard the like of it ever.

Anyway, he was able to identify the problem and fixed it, and that old "Bird" gave me no more trouble after that!

The following Scriptures and notes are to help you understand the reasons why I did what I did and why I said what I said.

There is a very challenging Scripture for us in *Matthew 17:20b,* *"So Jesus said to them, 'If you have faith as a mustard seed, you will say to this mountain, 'move from here to there,' and it will move; and nothing will be impossible for you."*

God has a way of getting your need met and your problem solved. That Way is discovered in your faith becoming a seed, which is called, "seed faith." When you plant a seed, God changes the nature of that seed so that it becomes a plant. The power of life surges in that tender young plant to such a great extent that even a mountain of earth cannot stop it from pushing upward!

Jesus says our faith in God is like a seed. When we put our faith into action, that is, when we release it to God, it takes on a totally new nature. It takes on the nature of a miracle in the making.

What is the mountain in your life? Loneliness, loss of a job, disease, a wounded relationship, trouble in your home? Something else? Be encouraged! Jesus shows the way to see that mountain removed!

First, God says that you have a measure of faith (Romans 12:3). It is resident within you. Second, God says that this faith comes alive by "hearing the Word of God" (Romans 10:17). Third, God says that you can apply your faith to see your daily needs met. How? You do something as an act of your faith. You sow the mustard seed—the smallness of your faith is sown into an action of love (Matthew 17:20). Then, when your faith has been planted and is growing, speak to your mountain and watch God set about its removal. (See 2 Chronicles 25:9 and John 10:10).

Man's economy fluctuates with the times and the seasons.

God's economy, however, has no shortages. God's supply always equals our need. He does not want any of His people to have any lack, but rather to "increase more and more" (see 1 Thess. 4:10-12). Do you think that if you give something to God, you will have less? Not according to God's "law of seed faith." When you give, you have just put yourself into a position of increase.

Faith that appears small or weak to us still can accomplish the humanly impossible. This mountain was a figure for any obstacle, hindrance, or humanly insurmountable problem—none of which is impossible for God. He works through committed people who accurately understand their authority and know His power, will, purposes, and provision.[15]

Scripture says in **Romans 10:10**, "*For with the heart one believes unto righteousness, and with the mouth confession is made unto salvation.*" **Matthew 12:34b** says, "*For out of the abundance of the heart the mouth speaks.*"

---

15 Ibid.

In *Genesis 1,* God spoke creation into existence. Whatever captures your heart in life, you will find yourself speaking about it. The power is not in the speaking but in the power of God. Speaking is a means to express that trust in Christ.

I hope that you will appreciate the need for me to give a scriptural basis for this story, or any of my other stories, because whatever I do, I base it all on Scripture.

Car Crash on the Moycullen Road

One day in 2003, while travelling out from Galway City to the village of Moycullen, I came across a car crash outside the house of someone I knew. I parked my own car a bit beyond the incident and went back to the site of the crash. I found that nobody was seriously injured, but my friend's niece and her mother were in that car. The other person involved in the crash, who was also familiar to me, was at her car window. I could see that this young woman was distressed, so I said to them, "Do you mind if I pray for you?"

They said, "Of course you can pray."

I laid my hand on the shoulder of the woman who was driving the car. I then invited the Holy Spirit to come and bring His peace to this situation, and I asked for God's rule and protection over everybody and everything concerning this accident in Jesus' name. There and then, the young woman driver slumped over the steering wheel. Her mother who was beside her became nervous because she did not know what had happened to her daughter. I said it was all right because the Holy Spirit was giving her daughter His peace and was ministering to all the tension that had built up concerning this accident. He was dealing with it, so not to be anxious. I left them in the capable hands of the Lord and went home.

About two weeks later, the young woman's uncle came to visit Geraldine and me, as we were doing business together. He did not know that I was the person who had been responsible for praying at his niece's accident.

I inquired about the accident and he began to tell us a story about which I had been unaware. He said that his niece had an accident outside his sister's house when, all of a sudden, a man appeared at her window and said, "Do you mind if I pray?" He did so, and left as quickly as he arrived. He said that before this man had come to pray, his niece and the man involved in the car crash had been fighting and arguing relentlessly. However, after this other man had come along and prayed, all the arguing and fighting stopped and peace came upon the whole situation. I could not resist it. I told him that I was the man who had prayed. My friend who had heard about this story was overawed by this reality. The power of prayer was demonstrated, along with the fact that I was the strange man who had prayed.

He was speechless, and we gave thanks and glory to the Lord. God's Kingdom had come into the situation and part of that kingdom is peace.

The Lord Preserved Me From Having my Ankle Severed From My Body

I had the task of mowing the grass on a two-acre site over a period of a few years, which meant I needed a riding lawn mower. There was a section of lawn that had grown too long to cut with the mower. This left me with the hard task of cutting the long grass with a scythe, and then it had to be gathered into small bundles. I then got my son, Simon, to operate the lawn mower and cut the remaining rough grass down to lawn size.

As he started to cut it, I watched him from a distance of about twelve feet away. I had a two-pronged hayfork in my hand and was leaning on it as I watched him cut the grass.

Suddenly we heard a loud bang coming from under the lawn mower, and then the hayfork on which I was leaning shivered in my hand. We did not know what had happened, but there was a huge indent on one prong of the hayfork. We turned off the engine of the lawn mower and looked underneath it. The blade had come loose and had been propelled out from under the mower like a bullet.

The Lord provided the shield for me in the two-pronged hayfork, which shielded my ankle from amputation, as my legs were behind it. We never found the blade, but my leg is in one piece. I am so grateful to the Lord Jesus.

The Healing of an Injured Dog

One day I was driving into the city with Geraldine, and as we got to the outskirts of the city, we came across an accident on the side of the road that had attracted a number of people. They all looked quite upset. For some reason, I felt I needed to stop the car and investigate what had happened. When I passed through the crowd, I discovered that it was a dog that was injured, and it was not in good shape at all. The dog was bleeding from its nose, and its back legs could not hold it up. The people did not know the dog or its owner, but I recognised the dog and knew the telephone number of its owner. Not long after I made the phone call, the owner arrived at the scene and proceeded to put the dog in his car. I led the way to the veterinary clinic. I went in with the owner and his dog whereupon investigation the vet told us that he had no hope for the dog, as his lungs appeared to be full of blood.

The dog's owner was distraught at hearing this terrible news. I knew that the Lord had me connected to this incident, so when I heard the negative words from the vet and seeing the owner so distraught, about his dog, the Lord filled me with compassion for this lovely animal. I spoke out in the presence of the vet, his nurse, and the owner, and said, "Do you mind if I pray for the dog first?" Nobody objected.

I laid my hands on the very sick dog. Jesus says in **Mark 16:18, "...they will lay hands on the sick, and they will recover."** I did what Jesus instructed and called upon Him by the power of the Holy Spirit to heal the dog and restore him to full health. I also prayed that the Lord would give the vet the wisdom and the skill necessary to bring restoration to this dog. I could see that the three people present had never heard or seen the likes of this prayer before. I then left the clinic.

Two days later, I heard that this little dog had returned home with his back leg in a sling. He eventually made a full recovery.

Praise God!

All I can say is that God moves in mysterious ways. He will use unusual ways to show His love and power. I am sure God was trying to show that family something of His love and His response to the prayer of faith.

God showed me something about being led by the Holy Spirit, being moved with compassion, and being sensitive to His will.

Chapter 11

Our Trip to the United States in 2003, Including a Visit to Niagara Falls

ANOTHER desire we had in our hearts was to go to the United States to see Geraldine's cousins in Cincinnati, Ohio, who were always asking us to visit them. They were always coming over here to see us and the wider family in Ireland. Having said all that, this story is minimally about our visit to the cousins, but majors on other more spiritually-based events. If we were to go to the United States, we also desired to see the Niagara Falls, but with our small income and four young children—ages sixteen, thirteen, eleven, and nine years—that was going to take a miracle.

So we had committed to the Lord in prayer a trip for ourselves to the United States. A Scripture in *Matthew 19:26* says, *"But Jesus looked at them and said to them, with men this is impossible, but with God all things are possible."* In this case, He was talking to His disciples about it being easier for a camel to go through the eye of a needle than for a rich man to enter the Kingdom of God.

In our situation, it was going to be impossible for us to go to the United States with the resources we had, but giving the situation to the Lord as we did, anything was possible. As well as that fact, I have found it amazing how the Lord orchestrates events and the way He puts people across our path to help make things happen for us. The important thing for us is to be attentive as much as possible to what God might be doing at any given time in our lives, and by His grace, recognise His provision regarding what we have prayed for.

Our trip was planned for June to July 2003. However, back in November 2001, the Lord had a pastor of a church from the United States in Nashua, New Hampshire, visiting Ireland. As he was entering Galway City, where we lived, he and his wife spotted a sign on the side of the road that read, "Galway Christian Fellowship welcomes you."

Upon seeing the sign, the Lord impressed upon his heart to call in and make contact with our pastor. Although unaware of his need for him to contact us, but in obedience to the Lord's nudging, he called in and got talking to our pastor. Our pastor in turn invited them to stay. Geraldine and I were operating a Bed & Breakfast business at the time, so we were called upon to offer hospitality to visiting guests and speakers who came to church. We were always happy to offer hospitality, as we loved to do it. Furthermore, we never knew what blessing was about to walk through our front door.

When this pastor, Paul, and his wife Sandy, visited our home, the Lord really bonded us all together and every one of us was blessed. We were so bonded with this couple that we said to them we would love to visit them in their church in Nashua. The Lord was at work in this situation. I do not think it had dawned on either Geraldine or me at this moment that the Lord was setting the stage for our own visit to the United States. We didn't realize that Nashua was within driving distance of the Niagara Falls. The seed was sown in our hearts. We both pondered over all that was happening and we were so excited in our hearts. We loved this couple and we wanted to see more of them.

The following year, in 2002, a young Christian woman from somewhere in the United States visited our church and ministered to us by singing some gospel songs. While she was singing, the Lord was touching our hearts. I cannot remember now what words she sang, but during her singing, God stirred both Geraldine and me again about going to the United States. We again felt that the Lord was making a way.

After the church service was over, we got talking to this young woman and discovered she was from New Hampshire and had occasionally visited the Grace Fellowship Church, where our friends, Paul and Sandy were senior pastors. She also ran a Christian summer camp for children about 50 miles north of Nashua. Both our hearts were jumping. I thought, "What if we offered our labour to the campsite for a few weeks? I could do maintenance work on the site, Geraldine could work in the kitchen, and the children would have the benefit of Christian camp for a few weeks."

We got in touch with Paul, Sandy, and the campsite leader to see if we could stay in the church's facility as guests, and if the campsite leader would hire us to work at the camp so our children could attend the summer camp. We got the green light from all concerned, and all that was left was to finalise dates.

In February 1999, Geraldine got the news that cancer was in her body. By 2002, she did not have the energy for the B & B work any longer, so we put the house up for sale, as we had to close the business. We were finding it hard to sell the house, but early in 2003, somebody began to show an interest in buying it. We thought that if we could sell it, we would have the money to pay for the trip. By March 2003, we were sure that this person was going to buy our house.

I made enquiries about the cost of return flights for two adults and four children. I could not believe my ears when I heard how cheap the flights were. You must remember that 9/11 disaster on the World Trade Center in New York had taken place about one and a half years earlier. The fact that there were so few people travelling made the cost of tickets about half price. As well as that, we were nearly positive about this man buying our house. With the cost of our tickets so low, I purchased the return flights for our holiday in June by credit card.

We discovered about a month later that this buyer had walked away from purchasing our house. We were devastated. We'd had the house on the market for nearly two years. We had spent money on the trip that we did not have, and had made the commitment to our holiday. Nevertheless, we continued with our commitment and went to the States. We thought that since we did not have the money, we would just visit Grace Fellowship in Nashua, the Christian camp, and the cousins in Cincinnati. That was a lot for people who had no money, but we said we were determined to sell the house and that in due course it would be sold. Then we could pay back our debts. We decided to forget about going to the Niagara Falls as that was over the top considering our circumstances.

We finally got going on our trip in the middle of June 2003 and arrived at Grace Fellowship where we met that lovely couple, Pastor Paul and his wife Sandy, and his staff and church members. They absolutely spoiled us and were so welcoming and hospitable. Out of the staff members, the Lord bonded us with another couple, Roger and Patty, who had children around the same age as our own children. We spent about a week in Grace Fellowship, getting to know these people and being ministered to through music, teaching, preaching, some wonderful prayer times and lovely friendships.

When the day came for us to proceed north to Camp Fireside, Roger and Patty's children wanted to come to the camp also, as they knitted together very well with our children. After clarifying with the camp that there was space for three extra children, we all proceeded to the camp. Roger and Patty had to return to Nashua, leaving their children with us at camp.

As planned, I helped with the maintenance of the camp while Geraldine helped with the cooking. We were only a few days at the camp when Geraldine, who was cleaning the leader's office, spotted a calendar on the wall. This was still showing the month of June, even though it was the month of July. This particular calendar had a Scripture verse for every month of the year written over the photograph area of the calendar. When she turned over the leaf of the calendar to the month of July, she could hardly believe her eyes because the verse on it spoke to her so strongly. It aroused in her again the desire that she had buried in her heart to see the Niagara Falls. Through this Scripture, she felt that God wanted to bless her and give her the desires of her heart. She was nearly breathless and awestruck, with what God was saying. Faith was beginning to rise up within her. I had better tell you the verse that was on the calendar before you burst. It was *Psalm 145:16: "The Lord does open up His hand and does satisfy the desires of every living thing."*

I had a little table mat once, and on it was written, "If you love something, set it free. If it comes back to you, it is yours. If it doesn't, it never was."

We need to be able to let the desires of our heart go out of our grip, otherwise the thing may become an idol, and we end up loving it more than we love the Lord. *Psalm 84:11* tells us, *"No good thing does He withhold from those who walk uprightly."*

Proverbs 10:22 tells us, *"The blessing of the Lord makes one rich, and He adds no sorrow to it."* It is the most precious, wonderful, securing thing to let the Lord be lord and Father of our life.

Both of us were able to let this trip to the Niagara Falls go from our hearts, and we knew that if He wanted us to see it, He would make a way for us to see it.

When Geraldine told me of the promise of God that was in *Psalm 145:16,* she began to get nervous and lose a bit of faith. However, when I saw it, faith rose up within me and I took hold of it and got motivated. We both prayed together and conversed with the Lord about the verse she had laid her eyes on. We said to Him that if this is a promise that you are actually speaking to us about, we embrace it and will proceed to arrange to see the Niagara Falls. We told the Lord what we thought we needed to be put in place for it to be accomplished. The list we made went as follows:

1. We needed a car to get us there.
2. We needed somebody to guide us there because we never drove in the States.
3. We needed the hospitality house in Nashua to be vacant for a night so that we could go from there and make it our base.
4. We needed camping gear for the overnight stay near the Niagara Falls.
5. We needed permission to be released from camp two days earlier than planned to get to the Falls, as we had pre-arranged a flight from Boston to Cincinnati to meet up with Geraldine's cousins.

Believe it or believe it not, the day after we had prayed about Niagara Falls, Patty arrived at the camp with runners in her hand for her children, as they left them back in Nashua and were in need of them. While Patty was eating with us, we asked how far it was to the Niagara Falls. She replied that it was about a ten-hour drive.

"Why?" she asked. "Are you thinking of going?"

We replied, "Yes."

Patty said, "I would love to come too, as I have never seen it."

That was one request answered—someone to be with us.

We asked, "Where could we get a car?"

She replied that they had a second car but had lent it out to another couple for a while. She said, "I might be able to get it back for a couple of days—let me check."

That was a possible answer to the car request. We asked if the hospitality house was vacant at Grace Fellowship. We were told at the beginning of our holiday that after our first week's stay in the hospitality house, it was going to be occupied all summer by other visitors, but we asked the question anyway. Patty said that she would ask about the car and the hospitality house and let us know. In the meantime, we went to the camp leader and told her how the Lord was leading us to get that visit to the Falls. We asked if it would be all right with her if we left two days earlier than scheduled since we had pre-arranged a flight to Cincinnati. The camp leader gave us the release.

Patty came back to us on the phone the next day, saying that she was able to get the car. Secondly, the hospitality house, which was supposed to be occupied all summer, was free because the people who were supposed to come never arrived! However, she said that she and Roger had looked at their finances and could not afford to go. We got despondent, but we prayed again and asked the Lord to release finances into Roger and Patty's hands.

Two days later, Patty rang us and gave us the news that blew us all away. She said, "This morning we got mail from the tax office, and when we opened it we saw that they have given us a tax refund cheque. Now we have enough to join you on your trip to the Niagara Falls."

Again, I quote a Scripture from *Matthew 7:7, "Ask, and it shall be given to you; seek, and you shall find; knock, and it will be opened to you."* That Scripture is in a present continuous tense, which means, "ask and keep asking."

We obeyed this Scripture in all these areas when we knew that the Lord was guiding us, and look at how He opened up the way and provided for our trip to be established.

"Our God is an awesome God. He reigns from heaven above with wisdom, power, and might. Our God is an awesome God." These words are part of a song we sing in church and they are true. We were seeing the reality of it. With respect to the camping gear we would need, we were able to buy two tents in Walmart at a very low cost. God provided everything we needed without much effort, as He was the one who initiated it!

We went back to Grace Fellowship in Nashua to gather ourselves together. Patty said that we would camp at Letchworth State Park near Niagara Falls. They call it "the Grand Canyon of the East," which was about seventy miles short of Niagara Falls. With all our bags packed and ready to go, three adults and seven children got on the road at the break of day. We had our walkie-talkies for each car so that we could communicate with each other. If either one of us got lost or lost sight of the other, we could still keep in touch. It was purely exhilarating, another adventure creating memories for us all as a family and living in God's provision. We could not waste time on the road, as we had a nine to ten hour drive time and then camp in the park before it got dark.

By God's grace, we made it to the park in time. We all had a great time putting the tents up, cooking food, and toasting marshmallows with biscuits and chocolate. We had the pleasure of a two-night stay there.

The following morning had us all up bright and early. We were waiting for the day we were to see the Niagara Falls. We got going after a very early breakfast, as we had a seventy-mile trip ahead of us before we got to the Falls.

There were many created areas where we could get a good look at the Falls. But the main event was to get on the boat, The Maid of the Mist, which brought us to the base of the water falls. We had all our rain gear on so that we could sense the thunder of the rushing water crashing down next to us.

When we came to the office where we paid for the trip on the boat, we got the impression that the cost of the trip was going to be too expensive for all of us. Since Geraldine was the one who really wanted to experience the boat, I did not mind too much if I missed it. She said that she and one child would go. She chose Matthew. Elena told us that she had prayed to the Lord and asked Him to have the price of the tickets at a level where we could all go on the boat. Geraldine was saying that if the tickets were over $10 each, only she and Matthew would go. It was the grace of God that none of the other children, Simon, Elena, or Jessica kicked up a fuss. When we got to the ticket desk, we discovered that they were less than half the price we were thinking, so we all got on and got to experience it.

It was a wonderful experience to get drenched with raincoats on, and to be so near to the hundreds of thousands of tons of water crashing down right beside us.

When that was over, we walked across the border to the Canadian side of the Falls and were able to see it all from another perspective. On that side, we were able to get very near to the water where it drops over the edge and crashes to the bottom. What memories, and so many photographs we have to prove it.

When our viewing for the day was over and we returned to the park where we were camping, the heavens opened and down came the rain so hard that you could hardly see ten feet away from you. In the United States, they call it a gully washer.

Wasn't it a godsend that it did not happen during our time at the Falls? God was so gracious to us. We got back to the park in time to view the canyon and it was breathtaking. The children of both families had really bonded well together, which was great.

That night, we had our food and games together and talked about what we had all experienced that day. We got to bed early enough, as the next day we were faced with a ten-hour drive home to Nashua. This trip was accomplished by early evening, when we were able to share our adventure with other church members. *I thank you so much, Lord.*

Pastor Paul Berube was excited about the whole adventure and said, "Michael, you made it!"

I replied, "Amen."

The next day we were driven down to Boston where we got a flight to Cincinnati, Ohio, to see Geraldine's cousins. It was pure delight to connect with them all. Some cousins had to travel a long distance to come and meet with us, which we were very grateful. They could not do enough for us. We had all family barbecue times together. Twenty-five of us went as a group to a baseball match, which enabled our cousins to receive a favour. The favour was that the officials flashed up on the screen, "We welcome the Cunningham family from Ireland." We could hardly believe our eyes when we saw it. Another time we were brought to a theme park with drop zone and roller coasters of all sorts, which were absolutely breathtaking for the children. I kept my feet on solid ground. This trip was a holiday we did not want to finish. We were blessed out of our socks, spoiled rotten by everyone during our visit to the United States. Sadly, all good things have to end. We had to go back home to the porridge (the mundane things of life), but we had filled a photographic album with the most wonderful memories.

Chapter 12

My Prayer Before Geraldine Died

THE Bible reveals that the person of the Holy Spirit has been the primary agent in the entire ministry of the Word throughout the centuries. He leads us into all truth. He recalls Scripture to our minds. He teaches us.

Two days before Geraldine died, the Holy Spirit recalled a Scripture to me, which came from *2 Kings 2:1-16.* It prompted me to pray in a certain way. Geraldine was very seriously ill and if the Lord was not going to heal her, she was going to die because she was rapidly failing in strength.

I will try to condense the relevant points of these verses for you.

The Lord was about to take up Elijah into Heaven by a whirlwind. Elisha who was to be Elijah's successor, had learned that Elijah would soon be departing. Elijah had called Elisha to take up his office. Elisha was determined to follow him since a dying person would often pronounce blessings on others. Elisha did not want to miss his moment of opportunity. He made one last request of Elijah—*a double portion* of Elijah's spirit, since a double portion was the privilege of the firstborn. Elijah had said to Elisha that he would only receive the double portion if he saw him depart.

Elisha realised that he did not have the capability to fulfill the awesome responsibility of carrying on Elijah's work. As Elijah's successor, Elisha applied the principle of the firstborn to ask for a spiritual inheritance. This is described as the Spirit of Elijah, and is either an indirect or a direct reference to the Holy Spirit. The Hebrew word for spirit has a wide range of meanings (it can refer to the human spirit, the Holy Spirit, an evil spirit, a prophetic gift, or even the wind.) Here it probably refers to the energising power of the prophetic spirit that characterised the life of Elijah. He, the Holy Spirit, is the author of Elijah's prophetic gift and the energising power of his ministry.[16]

Two verses affected me very strongly when reading this report.

Verse 9: Elisha said, "Please let a double portion of your spirit be upon me."

Verse 10: so he [Elijah] *said, "You have asked a hard thing. Nevertheless, if you see me when I'm taken from you, it shall be so for you; but if not, it shall not be so."*

As a small aside, the story of Elijah and Elisha here has a mirror image with the story of Jesus' Ascension into Heaven. You may find it interesting.

Jesus had informed His disciples that He had to leave this world to return to the Father, in order that the Helper, the Holy Spirit, could come to the Earth. Jesus told His disciples that greater miracles they would do in His name when He leaves. The disciples saw Jesus depart from this world on a cloud. Ten days later the promised Helper, the Holy Spirit came upon the disciples in the form of tongues of fire and empowered them to be His witnesses on this Earth.

It is interesting to note that when Jesus first came into His ministry, the people thought that He was Elijah returned.

That was a long but necessary introduction to my story. However, since it forms the basis of what I have to say, I had to give it to you.

When the Holy Spirit recalled this situation in Scripture to me, I knew what I needed to ask the Lord in prayer.

Geraldine had wonderful gifts of love, discernment and wisdom. I recognised these gifts in her and I knew I was trailing well behind in these qualities. I said to the Lord, "it looks like you are going to take Geraldine home to yourself, and I know you will not be taking her home in a chariot of fire. If I see her *last breath*

---

16 Ibid.

on Earth I'm asking you to give me the gifts of love, discernment and wisdom in greater measure than she had, as I will need them very much to cope with the task of bringing up the children you have given us. The Scriptures tell us, *'You have not because you ask not.'* Therefore, I am asking."

I knew that I had to engage with the Lord and ask Him for these gifts because I was going to be left alone to deal with everything.

Two days after I prayed this prayer, Geraldine died. I was by her side with both families when she left us. I saw her take her last breath and depart from this world. It was the saddest moment I had ever experienced in my life. It was the greatest loss of the most precious friend I had on Earth. This brought to an end all our companionship and closeness of spirit, soul and body. Her death was an immense wrench.

The day after we buried Geraldine I was put to the test regarding the three gifts I had asked of the Lord, as we had a bit of a mess at home. To everyone else's surprise—and mine—I did not lose my cool. I had the peace of God and knew the Lord had given me what I had asked for because previously I would have lost the plot. I would be shouting my head off and getting upset, and upsetting everybody else too. For my sake, and most of all for my children's sake, I needed to change and quieten down. I had been working through a lot of anger and frustration over the years, but the Lord had gotten me to pray this significant prayer for the well-being of us all, and those outside of my family as well.

Since the time I had prayed that very specific prayer, one of my daughters told me that she used to be afraid of me, simply because I always gave vent to shouting. Now she tells me that she was not afraid of me anymore. I was horrified to think that I had caused her to fear me, but immediately my heart melted when I heard that she no longer afraid. I was so grateful to God for what He was doing in me. I apologised to her for the fear I had inflicted upon her. Many times we fail to realise the full impact we have on our children because we are so caught up with ourselves and what is affecting us.

Another day when I was on the phone, telling this testimony to somebody, my other daughter was listening to my conversation. When I had put the phone down, she said to me that I have become like "two people in one." She meant that inside me one parent was hard and the other one soft. Now whom was she getting her experience from! I needed to change. My children needed me to change. My great sadness is that my precious wife did not experience the radical change in me before she died, even though I was calming down in good measure.

What strikes me very much here is that I only got this radical change when I was desperate and cried out to the Lord. For years, I was tolerating the old self and did not bother to take real stock of what I was like. Even though that area of my life was not demonstrating the character of Christ, I was ignoring it and careless about the call to demonstrate the character of Christ in my life.

For example, take the process of purifying gold. The gold has to be put into a furnace with flax, and in the intensity of the heat, the impurities are drawn to the flax, rise to the surface and are scooped away. Seven times the process will be repeated until the gold is pure and has a transparent look about it.

We have our times in the furnace of life—the heated moments in life when our soul is raging over something when filth such as anger, hatred, foul mouthing, envy, and backbiting come to the surface. These times are excellent opportunities for us to take stock of the rot that is in us. For many years, in the area of anger in my life, I did not do what I should have done. My family and I were the losers because of it. It was as though I did not invite the Holy Spirit (who is like the flax in the gold that draws the impurities to the exposed surface) into that area of my life.

When we do invite the Holy Spirit into an area of our lives, He will find a way of drawing the filth to the surface. Be sensitive and repent to God for the filth and surrender it to the Lord. Ask Him to take it away and cleanse you. Ask the Holy Spirit to seal your heart like closing the door in that area, so that it does not happen again.

This process will help us become more like Jesus. Moreover, after a season of doing this, we become more invisible and the character of Christ more visible in us. Bringing forth the *"fruit of the Holy Spirit, which is love, joy, peace, patience, kindness, goodness, faithfulness, gentleness, self-control. Against such there is no law"* (Galatians 5:22-23).

These virtues are characterised as fruit in contrast to "works." Only the Holy Spirit can produce them, and not our own efforts. Whereas the works of the flesh are plural, the fruit of the spirit is one and invisible. When the Spirit fully controls the life of a believer, He (Jesus) produces all of these graces. The first three concern our attitude towards God, the second triad deals with social relationships, and the third group describes principles that guide a Christian's conduct.[17]

The Lord has done something deep and profound in my heart, and I am so conscious that my life should glorify my Lord and Saviour as I grow more into the image of Christ. I am aware that if I were to shout now, as I did years ago, I would frighten myself. It seems so alien to me now to shout. I am so grateful and thankful to the Lord—by the Holy Spirit—for the real and tangible work He has done in my life.

I have spoken about my change in the area of love. As regards wisdom, I have stopped striving and being anxious about achievements in this life. I surrender all my desires to the Lord and I rest in the knowledge that He has a plan of welfare and works to do in my life. All I need to do is to be obedient to His promptings. I am living out of the peace of God. As long as I say "yes" to the Lord, I know He will not let something pass me by that He has for me.

Biblical wisdom unites God, the source of all understanding, with life, where the principles of right living are put into practice.[18]

---

17 Ibid.
18 Ibid.

James 3:13-18 instructs us in the difference between heavenly and demonic wisdom. I'll let you read it for yourself, but I will give you *verse 17, "But the wisdom that is from above is first pure, then peaceable, gentle, willing to yield, full of mercy and good fruits, without partiality and without hypocrisy."*

Therefore, when we are living in accordance with the ways written down in *verse 17,* we know we have received the wisdom that comes from God. It is absolutely liberating.

In regard to discernment, the Lord has opened up my eyes to many things, enabling me to judge and decide between things when I see them, and in a greater measure than before.

When we pray in the will of God, we receive answers from Him. What a wonderful heavenly Father we have, because when we ask Him for bread He does not give a stone or a serpent. To leave with a parting word here: Whatever concerns us, concerns God.

Chapter 13

A Tribute to My Wife, Geraldine — 6th August 2008

Born: 27th January 1959
Died: 2nd August 2008

Note: Some of this I have spoken of already in a previous chapter, but this is what I said at her funeral. I also added a bit more detail.

I thank you all for coming here today. I can see that Geraldine was greatly loved. I thank our Pastor Stephen Kenny for all his love and support to Geraldine over the last few years. I want to thank Geraldine's sisters, Mary, Ann, Patricia, Martina, and my brother David's wife, Mary for their round the clock outpouring of unselfish love and care for Geraldine over the last week of her life. I will treasure it always.

I thank all of you who upheld Geraldine in prayer over the past few years. I thank my own family for all their support to me and my children at this time as well, and for all who helped in making this funeral service possible.

I never knew Geraldine prior to her having a relationship with the Lord and being filled with the Holy Spirit.

I remember when she walked into Pastor Graeme and his wife Fran Wylie's sitting room during a prayer and Bible study meeting in early 1984. My first thought was "There is hope yet" but when her boyfriend followed her, I put closure to my first thought. However, due to circumstances changing and the Lord's directing that "first thought" became realised in marriage to Geraldine two years later.

For me to talk about Geraldine, I cannot but talk about Jesus as well. They were inseparable. Her love for God was greater than what her love was for me. I was only playing second fiddle and vice versa, and after we worked over a few humps, as I described earlier, we lived in perfect harmony.

She told me later that before she came to her first prayer and Bible study meeting, she told her friend that if she did not like it she would never come back again. For a person to go to a meeting that was outside the traditional form twenty-four years ago was a big thing and not easy to do. However, when she heard the gospel preached and taught by our pastor, Graeme, she embraced Jesus and the Word of God fully. She said this is what I have been waiting for all my life. She never stopped coming back after that. Having gained enough knowledge and understanding of God and His Word over the next few months, she put aside the leaning upon her own understanding. She placed her trust totally in God and confessed Jesus as Lord and Saviour. Jesus became to her **"Wonderful, Counsellor, Mighty God, Everlasting Father, and Prince of Peace" (Isaiah 9:6).**

The consequence of that action of trust and declaration, God saved her, gave her His Holy Spirit as a deposit for her eternal life and the power to live for Him while on Earth. With the Holy Spirit living in her, she had the assurance that when her body died, her spirit would rise to be present with the Lord forever.

What a heart of love Geraldine had for everyone she knew. No matter what anybody did that would hurt her, she would always choose to think the best. She would, as the Bible puts it, swear to her hurt and not change. She was a great challenge to me in that area. She was always looking out for someone who looked as if they needed comfort or encouragement. She give him or her Scripture to help them as well as being practical when the situation presented itself. She would always speak up for what was right in a firm but persistent and gentle way, and address something that was out of order. Whenever we had an extra bit of money, the first thing she would do was to plan its exit to other people in need.

Geraldine was a treasure of a wife to me given by God, and He used her to sort me out. In the early years of our marriage, she really did need that steel in her spine that God gave. She was an excellent mother to our children and stepson Marc. She gave them great roots and was in the process of giving them wings to fly.

Geraldine was also a great badminton player. She was like a cat at the net. I could well imagine her with her big bright eyes, and quick reflexes returning that shuttlecock back over the net. She has a few trophies to prove it as well.

She was a very good sprinter. The girl that won an Irish medal one particular year, she was able to beat; but during the trials, Geraldine tripped and fell in her race and missed the medal. Geraldine also loved running around the fields rounding up the sheep for her dad. She loved adventure and travelling. As a family, we managed a few lovely memorable adventures—one to Swedish Lapland to close friends we had there and another to the United States.

Cooking and experimenting with new dishes was really a pure joy to her. It was no wonder that with a gift of hospitality and a love for producing lovely food, both she and I ran a Bed & Breakfast business for many years.

We know that the fruit does not fall far from the tree. Geraldine's father was a builder, so it was no surprise that she had such a love for houses, architecture, interior decorating, and the buzz for business. There were so many of her talents she wanted to give expression. There was never a dull moment with her.

For many years, her one regret was that she never got to do an interior design course. The Lord made a way for her but sadly, due to the cancer and its treatment, she could not finish it, but that did not stop her.

The Scriptures indicate to us from **Psalm 37:4** that **"... if you delight yourself in the Lord He will give you the desires of your heart."** There was one desire we had as a couple and that was to design and build our own house. That dream began to come true four years ago and at a time when the cancer came back a second time and even more severely. However, that did not stop her. We designed our own house. I drew it up and built it by direct labour, and she had the greatest pleasure in designing the interior of the house with the resources we had at our disposal. She never wasted anything, and had a great gift of estimating accurately. Geraldine's favourite magazines were houses and gardens, so the garden and its flowers got serious attention and everything pertaining to that area was carefully planned out. Before she died, we got 90 percent of the house completed.

As Geraldine was in relationship with the Lord, she spoke to Him and Him with her, and that was through the Bible.

A week before she found the cancer lump she had been reading in **the Book of Joel**. It talked about great devastation, about what the gnawing locust, the swarming locust, the creeping locust, and the consuming locust had eaten. While reading this passage the Lord was impressing upon her heart that there would be great devastation coming but she also felt the Lord saying to her, "Hold on to my Word, hold on to my Word." She felt like saying those words ten times and on top of that, He also indicated to her to "Wrap my Word around your heart, even if it means a matter of life or death." She did not know whom this word was for, so she spoke it out in church thinking it might be for someone else, but no one responded to it. However, one week later, she found a lump that turned out to be malignant. She knew then that the Word had been for her, and that in His love for her He had forewarned and forearmed her and prepared her for what was to come.

A prophetic team of people came to our church in May 1995, and when addressing Geraldine, they saw a real depth and a real strength in her and establishment about her. Then in March 2000, a year after she got cancer, another prophetic team of people came to our church, and when they spoke to Geraldine, a member of the team saw great strength within her and they said, "And I just see you with someone as it were as a rod of steel in your backbone, that's not the normal steel you could bend, it's like a metal within you that is so strong, like that it has a strength within you that will not bend whenever adversity will come against you." These words were spoken to Geraldine from people who knew nothing of her in the natural sense, but were inspired by the Holy Spirit.

It showed me that God always confirms what He is doing and encourages us at the right time. The word that Geraldine received from **the Book of Joel** described one type of locust. That was the consuming locust, which should have indicated to her the outcome of this disease *but we did not perceive it like that, and the other words the Lord spoke to her left us wondering as to the outcome. However, we knew He was going to help her along the way.*

*To give us an idea as to how we are tested in life and to the spiritual activities that go on in the unseen realm, let us look at **the Book of Job** and Job himself. He was a righteous and blameless man, a God fearing man and who shunned evil.*

Job 1:68 *states:* **"Now there was a day when the sons of God (in this case it means celestial beings or angels God created as His servants) came to present themselves before the Lord, and Satan also came among them. And the Lord said to Satan, 'From where do you come?' So Satan answered the Lord and said, 'From going to and fro the earth, and from walking back and forth on it.' Then the Lord said to Satan, 'Have you considered my servant Job, that there is none like him on the earth, a blameless and upright man, one who fears God and shuns evil?'"**

Here Satan appears as "the adversary" to disturb God's Kingdom by causing trouble. Job is declared by God himself to be blameless and upright, and yet he is tried—not because of his unrighteousness but in spite of his righteousness. His trial was to establish his righteousness, as well as to give him deeper insight into his relationship with God and a greater understanding of his own nature. While Satan's goal was to prove Job to be a sinner, God's goal was to establish forever the sincerity of Job's faith. The trial is, in fact, a statement of God's faith in our faithfulness and integrity. When Job passed the trial, God blessed him twice as much.[19]

I see a great parallel here to Geraldine's situation. She was God's child anyway, destined for eternal life without any pain or suffering. God's ways and thoughts are not ours. We have to trust Him in all things. We do not fully know the purpose of her trial and death at such a young age, but a purpose there was and still is, and what God

---

19 Ibid.

wanted to fulfill out of it we will have to wait and see. His grace is always sufficient. In her trial, like Job, she never cursed God. Whatever trial Geraldine was going through, I believe she passed it, and like Job, her trial had nothing to do with any unrighteousness.

There is a promise in the New Testament in **1 Corinthians 10:13,** **"No temptation (it refers to trials as well) has overtaken you except such as is common to man; but God is faithful, who will not allow you to be tried beyond what you are able, but with the trial will also make the way of escape, that you may be able to bear it."**

All of these nine and a half years of her battle with cancer; Geraldine did what God told her to do by holding on to His Word. She also wrapped His Word around her heart. Repeatedly the Lord sustained her, flooded her with His peace, encouraged her with His Word, and strengthened her by His Spirit.

Four and a half years ago, when she got secondary bone cancer, she began to plan her funeral. She received prayer from a pastor from another church. He was not told what was wrong with Geraldine. In prayer, he broke off chains of oppression around her along with other things that he addressed. After the prayer, she never had thoughts of planning her funeral again. Praise God. Every time the devil came to steal her God-given peace or to try to destroy her walk with the Lord, she drew from God's sustaining Word or she received prayer.

Geraldine lived in victory over this cancer, died in victory, and had God's peace all the way. After all, cancer is only spelled with a small "c" and Christ is spelled with a big "C."

I showed her a Scripture some weeks ago, which I felt God quickening to me. I showed her the Scripture and through that Scripture, God gave her hope in her heart that she would come out of hospital (that place of captivity) alive. Last Tuesday, 29th July, God honoured that Word she had received into her heart a few weeks earlier when we brought her home, alive. That hope based on Scripture did not disappoint her.

From the promise given in **1 Corinthians 10:13.** I knew that when Geraldine came to the place of not being able to take any more of this, God was going to do one of two things. He was either going to heal her or take her home. We now know that His plan for her was to take her home. Geraldine and I prayed together two weeks ago when she could not take any more treatment. We both asked God for the last time to raise her up out of this in Jesus' name, and if He was not planning to heal her, that He would take her home swiftly. That, He surely did. Ten days later she died.

I did enough prayer battle to know the devil was out of this situation. I am at peace knowing that it was God who took her home and that it was not the devil robbing her of life. On Saturday morning about 11:45 a.m., our present pastor, Stephen Kenny, came to check in on Geraldine. She was not in good shape at all. Martina, Geraldine's sister asked Stephen to read a Psalm. Stephen read **Psalms 1, 23** and **25**. He closed the Bible and felt enough had been said. Twenty seconds later my precious wife, Geraldine took her last breath and is now dwelling in the house of the Lord forever.

I thank you, Lord, for giving me the privilege of knowing such a woman.

Chapter 14

A Possible Air Crash Averted Through Prayer

AFTER my wife, Geraldine died in August 2008, I thought it important to arrange a family holiday. I felt it would bond my family together and help ease the grief we had experienced following her death. I arranged in October 2008 for our trip in June 2009. The fact that the holiday was arranged so far in advance gave us a focus—something to look forward to.

My son, Marc, lives in Australia, and we were reuniting with him for six and a half weeks. My second son, Matthew was to be with Marc from March 2009, so I was to bring my third son, Simon, and my two daughters, Elena and Jessica, with me. As we were travelling half-way around the world, it seemed a good idea to include a trip to New Zealand for a week as well. The entire round trip meant that we included ten flights in all.

No sooner had I arranged the trip in October 2008, when fear struck my heart. *What if there was an air crash on one of these flights?*, I thought. If that happened, most of the family would be wiped out in an instant. So I handed that fear to the Lord as it was not mine to possess, and asked Him to advise me if it was safe for us to proceed with the holiday or not. I was willing to stay at home, lose the money, and be safe, rather than go and be injured, or worse, killed.

While waiting for God's response, every fibre of my being was on red alert, expectant that I would hear back from Him. Sure enough, about three weeks later, the Lord spoke to me and gave me His answer as I was reading *Psalm 118:17.* With the Word of the Lord in my heart, my fear was immediately cancelled out. The verse said, *"I shall not die, but live, and declare the works of the Lord."* I told the Lord, "Thank you so much for this Word.

Since my family and I are not going to die, I shall proceed with the plans as they are."

However, to declare the works of the Lord means that something has to happen for me to declare. Even with the knowledge that something unknown was going to happen, I was without fear, because I had that knowing now and the assurance that the Lord was going to keep us safe. I was at ease because my trust was in Him.

We started our journey on June 24, 2009. I always include the Lord in all my activities, as I know from experience that when you invite Him, He is there for you. Our first flight from Cork to Heathrow was uneventful. At Heathrow, we worked our way through each terminal until we got to terminal four, where we were due to board our next flight. When we got to the waiting room, I got this need in my heart to know the identity of the aircraft we were going to sit in for the next thirteen hours. However, I was not fearful, but at peace. After making a few enquiries, the aircraft was identified and as soon as I looked at it, the Lord alerted me and told me to pray for it. My prayer went like this: "Lord, if there is anything in the aircraft that is malfunctioning, make it known. I also ask that the person who might see the malfunction will not be careless about it, but will be awake and careful to make sure it is corrected, In Jesus' name." I did not pray out of fear, but from the prompting in my heart from the Lord.

A short time later, we all boarded the aircraft, and when we were all seated, the captain spoke to us and apologized to us on two counts for the time delay in taking off. First, "the aircraft was late coming in from another flight," which was acceptable, and second, "just as you were being seated, we discovered that there is a malfunction with the fuel pipes." I immediately gave thanks to the Lord. My trust in and prayer to the Lord was being rewarded. It took three and a half hours to fix the malfunction with the fuel pipes, and all of that time we were left sitting in the cabin without any air conditioning.

When the malfunction was repaired, the captain came back and told us that the flight would now proceed to its destination. He had no sooner said that when the Lord alerted me again and prompted me to pray concerning the aircraft a second time. I did so. I said, "Lord, if there is any other hidden malfunction on this aircraft make sure that it is exposed before we lift off the runway, in Jesus' name." I sat there trusting Jesus, as the airplane taxied out to the runway. We reached the start position, straightened up, the engines were put on full power, and we started moving, feeling the G forces as it moved. After travelling about 300 meters, the brakes were suddenly applied and we knew that something else had gone wrong. The captain spoke to us again, apologized, and said that when they had applied full power to the engines a warning light came on in the dashboard indicating that the cargo door was malfunctioning. They needed to pull over to terminal five and investigate the condition of the cargo door. That was close! We had nearly left the runway.

I said to the Lord, "Once again, thank you so much for what you have done in saving us from a possible disaster, but Lord, I am not at ease about continuing this flight on this aircraft. I ask you to get us off this aircraft and arrange for us to continue the journey on another aircraft." After waiting for thirty minutes, the captain spoke to us again and said that they were not having any success with the cargo door. "We are going to disembark this aircraft and arrange to get you another aircraft." Twenty hours later, we embarked on another aircraft and proceeded with the journey, and my trust in the Lord increased even more. This experience with the Lord had a profound impact on my life. Even though I had known Him and His faithfulness over the previous twenty-six years, this was a new development!

During my holiday in Australia, I saw three TV programmes on aircraft disasters. If I did not have God's reassuring promise from the Scriptures that I was going to be safe, I know that the devil would have jumped on my back and tried to whisper terror into my heart and mind. Nevertheless, praise God, I was able to look at the programmes and still keep God's perfect peace.

When I returned home from our holiday, I happened to look at a programme on TV and watched one man who was reporting that an aircraft had crashed with serious consequences just because the cargo door had not shut properly. As I watched, I thanked the Lord again.

I do not know if anybody else responded to the Lord's prompt to pray for the aircraft. But if nobody else did and I was the only person to hear His call, and if I had not prayed as I should have done when the Lord prompted me, perhaps all of the 300 people on the aircraft could have had a very serious accident in mid-air with great devastation. Who knows? As I said at the beginning, in order to declare the works of the Lord something has to happen to make this declaration. Well, something did happen and we saw the saving power of the Lord who protected us from a possible disaster. His promised Word did prove true.

We need to be careful not to have too many distractions occupying our minds and drowning out the sound of the still small voice of the Lord. The Lord is gentle, and He does not shout at us to get our attention. Had I worn earphones in my ears, listening to either the radio or music, I might have missed God's prompt to me to pray for the aircraft, as my ears and heart would have been tuned into another frequency.

There is a spiritual world—a world unseen to the naked eye—and it dominates our natural world. We all come under its influence. On one side, you have God who loves us, who made us, and who wants us safe and saved. On the other side you have Satan who is totally opposed to God's plan for our lives and whose sole aim is to destroy, steal, and kill. With that in mind, we need to be on the alert and submit ourselves to Jesus.

It struck me afresh that, even though God can do all things, He includes us in what He wants to do, so He prompts us in our hearts and minds and tries to get our attention to respond to His call for prayer. When we do, He responds and brings into being what was on His heart in the first place. He has given us a free will, so we can either accept Him or reject Him. That line He will never cross over without our invitation. When we do not pray and invite the Lord into our situations, we are in essence leaving ourselves open and bare, without any protection to the attacks of the devil. Jesus said in **Matthew 28:18, "All Authority has been given to me in heaven and on earth."** But we must remember the free will boundary line He has put in place. Therefore, when we invite the Lord into our life and our situations, we bring in His authority and rule, which encompasses Heaven and Earth. Thus, we are safe, and then He overrides any attack or activity of the devil that is against us. Jesus spoke of the devil in **John 10:10** saying. **"The thief does not come except to steal, and to kill, and to destroy. I have come that they may have life, and that they may have it more abundantly."**

Jesus is truly a Saviour, a deliverer, an everlasting Father who cares for us more than we could ever imagine. He promises in **the Book of Jeremiah 29:11, "For I know the thoughts that I think toward you, says the Lord, thoughts of peace and not of evil, to give you a future and a hope."** It is important to listen to God, to pray to Him according to His Word. It is profitable to obey Him and sometimes like this situation, it is imperative if a matter of possible life or death is in the balance. I am forever grateful to Him.

God is Good all the Time!

Chapter 15

Overexposure to the Australian Sun

O N Saturday morning, 15th January 2011, after spending three weeks with my son in Perth, we went to the swimming pool to have a swim and rest in the sun for a while. On all the previous occasions when I was out under the sun during the holiday, I made sure I covered my skin with the correct sunblock. However, this morning I was careless and thought I had enough of a base tan on at this stage, so I relaxed about applying any suntan cream on my skin. Top of that, I failed to put on my hat and sunglasses. It was sheer madness and nothing less. We spent about two hours under the midday sun between having some swims and sun bathing. I knew at this stage I had put myself in danger and when we got home I noticed that my skin was red raw.

That night I got a sting under my left eye, which quite concerned me, and with my skin so dry, it absorbed nearly a half a bottle of moisturising gel. The next morning I went to the chemist shop and got some eye drops. The chemist said that if my eye got blurred vision it would be necessary to go and see the doctor. Thankfully, my vision did not get blurry. From that day until Monday afternoon when I flew home, my skin was not able to take any sun, and even under my clothes, my skin was stinging.

During my flight home and with the concerned state I was in, I talked to someone about my dilemma. The person told me that midday is the worst time of the day to go out because the UV rays are the strongest. I should have kept my mouth shut, as it did not help me to hear all this. The long flight home and sitting in the air-conditioned planes did not help either. I was very aware that I had a battle on my hands. I had a real worry that I might get cancer in my eye and throat since I was having dry sensations there as well. Somebody told me to give myself a few days to recover from it all, but the devil never lets up if he thinks he has half a chance with you.

On Wednesday night just having returned home, I had a dream. Suddenly I was aware of a man with an evil smirk on his face. When our eyes connected, this man said, "Got you," and with that, I felt my whole body full of goose bumps. I felt attacked and that something was attaching itself to me. I then started to pray and quoting the Scripture from *James 4:7, "Therefore submit to God. Resist the devil and he will flee from you."* Therefore, I rose up in my spirit and submitted myself to God. I gave Him thanks that my life was in His hands, and that all authority and power is given to Jesus in Heaven and on Earth. I thanked Father God that I was His child and filled with His Holy Spirit, and that He gave me authority in the name of Jesus because I was under His authority. I was in a panic and at the same time trying to keep my head right.

With that, I began to speak and I resisted the adversary that was trying to latch itself on to me by attacking my thinking, telling me that I had cancer. I ordered this evil spirit off me and shook it off. I kept shaking it off until I felt the presence of God with me, and Him routing the enemy. I quoted Scripture from *Isaiah 54:17, "'No weapon formed against us shall prosper, and every tongue which rises against you in judgement you shall condemn. This is the heritage of the servants of the Lord, and their righteousness is from Me,' says the Lord."*

I bound myself to the Lord and I loosed myself from the lies of the devil, and told him to stop whispering lies into my ear. I condemned his accusations in Jesus' name. My body calmed down after that. The Lord was making me aware that I got too alarmed if I thought something was going wrong with my body like the possibility of cancer in this case.

I gave thanks to God for His promise in *1 Corinthians 10:13,* which I have quoted in the previous chapter, where it speaks about not being tried beyond what we're able to deal with. Even though I had calmed down a lot, I knew the enemy was still lurking in the shadows. I believe as well that when we are fearful we are quite liable to draw things upon ourselves that have no right to be there. Because I was in a state of fear and alarm, my mind was working overtime, thinking that this sensation and that dryness was cancer. On Saturday morning, 22nd January, while still in my bed, I prayed to the Lord and said, "Lord, I choose not to fear."

I knew from Scripture through the Book of Job that the devil could do nothing unless the Lord allowed it. I realised that the Lord wanted me free indeed and to be so alarmed about this physical disease was not possessing total freedom. He allowed this, knowing how I was going to respond to it. The question is how could I ever minister faith or healing to anybody else if I was going to be gripped with fear in this area? It just had to be dealt with. ***Philippians, 1:28*** says, ***"And not in any way terrified by your adversaries, which is to them a proof of perdition, but to you of salvation, and that from God."***

This showed me that it was very important for me to live in the peace of God, and if I did not have it, I was to search the Scriptures until I found God's promise that would cancel out the particular fear I may have had.

Fear is essentially trusting in the devil. Here is an acronym for the word fear:

F: = False

E: = Evidence

A: = Appearing

R: = Real

It was vital for me to repent of being in the state of fear and allowing terror to reign in my life if I was to walk into the freedom that the Lord gives in this matter. If I did not stop fear dominating me, the devil would conquer over me and have his way with me, as the Scripture above indicates. Therefore, I chose not to fear anymore after I had entrusted this situation to Him, and to trust Him from then on. That meant for me simply to calm down. There is a Scripture that guides us in what to do with this matter. It is in ***Philippians 4:6-7, "Be anxious for nothing, but in everything by prayer and supplication with thanksgiving, let your requests be made known to God; and the peace of God, which surpasses all understanding, will guard your hearts and minds through Christ Jesus."***

This was God's instruction for me when in a state of anxiety or fear. I could not afford to stay in that condition, rather I was to give it to God. Spend time reading and absorbing the promises of the light of God's Word until the darkness—the lie extinguished. Otherwise, the devil would have had his way with me.

How do we dispel natural darkness? We all know how to do it. We turn on a light.

How do we dispel spiritual darkness? We get and apply the light of the promises of God's Word and the enemy has to flee. The Word of God is our sword, as we will find out in ***Ephesians 6:17***. It is beneficial to you to read the verses there from ***10-18.***

When we believe something in our heart, we will speak it out. I was active in verbalising my prayers to the Lord. As I believed, thus I spoke. When we are ignorant of the Word of God, the devil can and does run riot over our lives because we have nothing to fight him. That is why he wants to keep us ignorant of God's Word all the days of our life; he does not want to lose his control. We shall not let him deceive us another day.

Therefore, as soon as I had applied the instructions that were in ***Philippians 4:6-7*** to my situation, I was amazed at how my mind and my body calmed down.

The devil attacks our thinking first and if he succeeds there, he is a long way down the road towards destroying us. In this attack on my thinking, which was threatening my health, I believe we can draw sicknesses upon ourselves if we receive those lies and let them grow in our thoughts. Therefore, to strengthen myself in the Lord, it was imperative for me to remind myself of other Scriptures that God had spoken to me and had not yet come to pass. Thus, it gave me hope for the future.

Over the previous few months, God had been speaking to me and preparing me in the area of vision and destiny. This was giving me hope for the future. The Lord gave me a promise in *Jeremiah 29:11, "For I know the thoughts that I think towards you, says the Lord, thoughts of peace and not of evil, to give you a future and a hope."*

To be inflicted with cancer in the eyes and throat would be a calamity for me. It would kill stone dead any possibility of future ministry for the Kingdom of God through me, as God has given me a good singing voice and a gifting in evangelism and encouragement. Can you see the battle that went on to get me thinking contrary to the Word of God?

In *John 10:10,* Jesus says, *"The thief* [the devil] *does not come except to steal, and to kill, and to destroy. I have come that they may have life, and that they may have it more abundantly."*

I was still at the place of not knowing if I had done any serious damage to myself or not, but one thing I knew was that I had the peace of God. When I had that, the enemy could not triumph over me.

I realised that there was a stronghold of fear gripping my life with respect to ill health and particularly nasty ill health such as cancer attacking my body.

God promises us in *Romans 8:28, "And we know that all things work together for good to those who love God, to those who are the called according to His purpose."*

Vanity was at work in me, and I was not prayerful when I was careless about not putting on sunblock or wearing sunglasses under the Australian sun.

The devil wanted to damage me. The sun stung me. I got in a panic, but in that panic, I ran to God. He then showed me that I needed release from this stronghold of fear about being in ill health. When I submitted to God and resisted the devil, God brought freedom to me in this area of my life. *Galatians 5:1* says, *"Stand fast therefore in the liberty by which Christ has made us free, and do not be entangled again with a yoke of bondage.*" I won a battle, but I really had to apply the light of God's Word of promises to the situation and then put my trust in Jesus and calm down.

The enemy can only do to us what God or we allow him to do. For those who have not yet come to faith in Christ or are not yet engaged in spiritual warfare as Paul defines in *Ephesians 6,* if you find yourself in spiritual warfare, it's a sure sign of life. I went from being in a state of alarm and panic to a place of resting in God's peace. However, I was still concerned, which was also necessary because it kept me moving towards discovery. I had to remind myself that my life was in His hands.

I trust that the stronghold the devil had is gone. I know I have learned something very significant here. There may be a foothold of the enemy, but my aim, as is God's, is that the enemy will have no hold in this or any other part of my life. I will only know this when or if another attack comes my way again.

A couple of days after I had prayed and had this breakthrough, I met an old acquaintance of mine whom I had not seen for twenty years. During the course of our conversation and of all the topics of conversation he could have chosen, he started talking about close relatives—one of whom died of melanoma on the neck and another who had cancer in the nose and eyes. By the grace of God, I was able to listen to this report without getting nervous or alarmed inside myself, especially as I was battling with thoughts of cancer in the very same areas of my body as this man's relatives. Then, to make it worse, he drew closer to my face and said with a concerned countenance. "Are you okay? How are you doing?"

I said to him, "I think I'm doing okay."

However, before I answered him I was saying in my mind, "Get out of my face, Satan." It was not that this man was Satan. However, Satan was influencing him to speak about the cancerous conditions of his relatives to me. On top of that was the manner in which he had asked me about myself, because I was still not totally out of the woods regarding my own dilemma. The devil was using him just to instill fear and terror into me, to get me to live, act, and think contrary to God's Word. As Scripture indicates to us in **Proverbs 18:21, "Death and life are in the power of the tongue..."** The devil certainly knows the power of the tongue and he influences people to speak for his destructive purposes.

The next day, I visited my nutritionist because I was still in need of an answer to all the dry sensations I was suffering because of my overexposure to the sun. I asked her what she thought or if she had any answers for me.

She told me that I had gotten an overdose of Vitamin D and that the strange sensations would fade away shortly. I was so grateful to God that I had won the battle in my mind through prayer before I had received the answer to my problem from the nutritionist. I gained ground and got one step closer to greater freedom. Her words calmed me down and the devil's torment was over. I began to recover as she gave me some liquid herb to take which would bring some moisture back to my dry and damaged surfaces.

We are in a war zone, and Christ gives us victory if you are in Him and obedient to His Word.

Chapter 16

Life After Geraldine's Death

I AM writing this chapter three and a half years after Geraldine's death. Without a doubt, it has been the most traumatic period of my life, and that is putting it mildly. It was as though my soul went through a paper shredder. I have been struggling to keep my physical health in some sort of shape ever since. Whenever I try to get one physical ailment sorted out another malady shows up. That has been going on these past few years. In the midst of all this, I was nearly wiped out financially due to a project that Geraldine and I were both involved in that went pear-shaped. There were some things that we did not get fully right and this was one of them. Even with this serious setback, God held my hand. There is a comforting word in *Psalm 37:24, "Though he fall, he shall not be utterly cast down; for the Lord upholds him with His hand."*

I was severely challenged in my soul with many issues of the heart to overcome. If I did not deal with them correctly, there would have been spiritual consequences arising out of the situation. However, there are two sides to every coin. The first side of this coin shows all the struggles. The other side of the coin shows it has also been the most ground-breaking period of my life, especially because of the new mind-set God has given me, which will become apparent as I proceed through this chapter.

Two days after Geraldine died and before we buried her, I woke up one morning and thought someone had hit me on the head with a hammer. For the first three months, I was depressed. It took me until two to three o'clock in the morning to get to bed. I was finding something to occupy me all the time and had no desire to go to sleep, and then when I was in bed I never wanted to get out of it. However, I had four children to get to school each morning and to look after in general.

Another thing I noticed was that my memory and retention

span were affected. I had to get a notebook and write down everything I had to do because I could not rely on my brain to remember things. I was talking to someone one day, and mid-stream through our conversation I just walked off and left him wondering. I got back to him later and apologised for my conduct. I even found that when I was talking to somebody, and in the course of our conversation if the other person broke in on what I was saying—which is normal—I tried to restart the conversation again, I would not have a clue what I had been talking about ten seconds earlier. Some people close to me thought I was losing my memory, but I told them that this was part of the bereavement process, and it only comes to pass.

It took a little over a year for it to pass and the Lord restored that memory back to me. I must be all right now as I am writing this book! He has helped me recall many of the different testimonies I have written about, but having said that, most of the testimonies were cemented in my brain as I have talked about them a lot to people over the years. Nevertheless, I asked the Holy Spirit to help me with recall and He did.

The isolation was very difficult. Some people would ring or text me, but it did not offer the comfort one gets when somebody is physically present. It only personified the loss and absence of my late wife. I wondered if I had any friends in this world and I was beginning to think, maybe I had a deadly disease.

In those early days after Geraldine died I had great need to talk to somebody, but all I had were the four walls of the house, and you know what kind of response you get from those!

In this state of isolation and loneliness, I struggled greatly. I did not curse God or anybody, even though I had a sense that the devil wanted me to curse God and by so doing inflict serious damage upon my soul. However, God had His hand upon my life, and what the devil meant for harm, He has brought good out of it. I drew really close to God. I discovered in greater depth the truth of Him and Him being my Saviour, redeemer, and everlasting Father, wonderful Counsellor, my ever-present help in time of need. The one who never leaves me or forsakes me. The Holy Spirit who comforts me and leads me into all truth, whose Word is a lamp unto my feet and a light unto my path. Whose plans for me are for welfare and not for calamity, for a future and a hope. I relied on Jesus for everything and I was not disappointed. He was, and still is, so faithful. I realised in a deeper way His closeness to me and I was discovering that whatever concerned me, concerned Him. I was also discovering that He was the defence of my life. He was answering my cries, and I was becoming very aware of His loving watchful eye on every aspect of my life. It changed me forever.

In my isolation, I hurt an awful lot and I knew that offence was pounding on the door of my heart, but I knew where this offence came from. It is a spirit of offence.

> *Satan is cunning and crafty. Do not forget he can disguise himself as a messenger of light. If we are not trained by the Word of God to divide rightly between good and evil, we won't recognise his traps for what they are. Offence itself is not deadly—if it stays in the trap. But if we pick it up and consume it and feed on it in our hearts, then we have become offended. Offended people produce much fruit, such as hurt, anger, outrage, jealousy, resentment, strife, bitterness, hatred and envy. Some of the consequences of picking up an offence are insults, attacks, wounding, division, separation, broken relationships, betrayal and backsliding. Often those who are offended do not even realise they are trapped. They are oblivious to their condition because they are so focused on the wrong that was done to them. They are in denial. The most effective way for the enemy to blind us is to cause us to focus on ourselves.*[20]

Knowing where this offence comes from and its consequences if taken up, I fought hard against it and resisted it but I had

---

20 John Bevere, *The Bait of Satan* (Lake Mary, FL: Creation House, 1994).

my struggles. I submitted myself to God and I kept on forgiving people, thinking the best of them, but also knowing the reality of an enemy whose sole aim is to steal, and to kill and to destroy me spiritually. After some time I got back to serving people as best as I could. There were some good days and some not so good days but I knew I was gaining ground. After all, my soul as it were was like going through a paper shredder. I knew God was in the process of restoring my soul.

I knew the devil was putting fierce pressure on me to come to the place of giving up. And guess what? If I did do that, I would have given the thief a victory over my life and he would have knocked me out of service in God's Kingdom, just where he would love me to be, without threat to his domain anymore.

My reliance on people had gone. It was wrong of me in the first place to put so much reliance on people because we all have our fears, failings, pressures of all sorts a variety of mindsets, and so forth. My focus was too much on people to look after me rather than looking to the Lord for that. The Lord wanted that changed and I realized it. I learned a lesson in a very difficult way and I repented to God for my attitude to Him and to others. I was turning to God for everything and talking to Him as though there was nobody else on Earth. In addition, for a time it felt as if there was nobody else on Earth. It was the start of something wonderful and *new*.

The Lord brought me to a place of forgiving *all* whom I had perceived had let me down. I soon discovered that it was a universal problem for people who were severely sick or bereaving a death. The outside world leaves them alone, simply because the situation confronts their own fears of the illness the person may be having. When someone is bereaving, others do not know what to say nor do. They feel awkward and inadequate so, they stay away.

All I wanted for the first few months after Geraldine died was for someone to visit me, just to listen to me. I can only speak for myself here, as I know other people in the same situation who do not want to talk to anybody. It is important to speak and not bottle up our emotions—we only damage ourselves by not speaking. When nobody is coming to us, we need to go and find someone close enough to us who knows what we might need, who has patience and has a good pair of listening ears. Having said that, it is not easy to go while in that raw state because we just want to stay within our own surroundings.

There is a promise in the Scriptures that kept me sustained through all of this season. It is in *Romans 8:28, "And we know that all things work together for good to those who love God, to those who are the called according to His purpose."* I know I am repeating myself here but it is applicable to repeat it again.

The Scripture really blessed and comforted me. God said:

1. All things
2. Those who love God
3. To those who are the called according to His purpose.
4. I knew I was and still am part of the called people of God. Somebody once told me that when you look into a room through the keyhole of a door, you see a very small portion of the room inside. God does not allow us to see the full picture of our lives for our own safety. If we did, we might never want to get out of the bed in the morning. That is why we just have to trust Him when we do not see the full picture.

I did not understand why He took my wife home so early in her life. I did not understand all this isolation. However, God's promise to me was that *"in all things He was working out something for good."* I still trusted God. Job said in *Job 13:15, "Though He slay me, yet will I trust Him."* God had a purpose for my life and it was time for me to grab hold of it.

When Jesus becomes lord of our lives, He gives us a purpose for living. It is not our will, but His will be done in our lives.

The Apostle Paul writes in *2 Corinthians 4:7-12* about being cast down but unconquered:

> *Verse 7: "But we have this treasure in earthen vessels, that the excellence of the power may be of God and not of us.*

Verse 8: we are hard—pressed on every side, yet not crushed; we are perplexed, but not in despair;

Verse 9: persecuted, but not forsaken; struck down, but not destroyed—

Verse 10: always carrying about in the body the dying of the Lord Jesus, that the life of Jesus also may be manifested in our body.

Verse 11: for we who live are always delivered to death for Jesus' sake, that the life of Jesus also may be manifested in our mortal flesh.

Verse 12: So then death is working in us, but life in you."

Let's review:

In verse 7: Treasure—the knowledge of God in the face of Christ. Earthen vessels are weak and fragile. This verse is virtually thematic for the entire letter, expressing the paradox of how weak human beings can be the instruments of the power of God.

Verses 8-9: The providential hand of God was controlling Paul's persecutions, keeping them with manageable proportions.

Verses 10-11: Paul enlarges the theme of power through weakness to include life through death. However, in the midst of his perils he could experience the life of Jesus, strengthening and sustaining him in the present weakness and assuring him of future resurrection.[21]

I can identify greatly with these verses of Scripture. I was at a very weak and vulnerable time of my life. The devil tried to destroy me but Christ has raised me up out of it to become a better and stronger man.

"It's in the tough times that true character is forged, the life of Christ is reproduced in us, and our flimsy theology

---

21 Notes from Spirit-Filled Life ® Bible.

is exchanged for a set of convictions that enable us to handle things, rather than trying to escape from them.

"It's when the bottom drops out, and life tries to pound you into a corner of doubt and unbelief, that you need what perseverance produces: (1) willingness to accept whatever comes, (2) determination to stand firm, and (3) insight to see God in it all. Without that, we stumble and fall, and God is grieved. With it, we survive and conquer, and God is glorified."

Charles Lindberg said, "Success is not measured by what a man accomplishes, but by the opposition he encountered, and the courage he maintained in his struggle against it."[22]

In pressing into and drawing close to the Lord, I was discovering a joy that I did not have before. I was searching deep into God's heart and character through His Scriptures. I was being anchored more in Him and the things that were shaking around me were not phasing me out. God was speaking new things to me, opening up Scripture to me, even Scripture that I had known many years ago but this time they were penetrating home to me. I needed Him desperately. He has the words of eternal life and He responded to my deep need and my cries to Him.

Autumn 2010, I was at a very low point. I felt emotionally and physically battered and thought that the next stop for me was the grave. Moreover, I did not mind it at all. However, the Lord had impressed upon my heart to go to Dublin and listen to a Pastor Joe Corry. When I got there, he happened to be speaking on vision and destiny. I said to myself, that if the Lord has me listening to this message, the grave is not for me yet! Therefore, I shook myself and paid great attention to what the Lord was saying to me through this man. I started receiving purpose, vision and hope for my future because I was beginning to realise that there was a future for me,

22 Bob Gass, *Discovering Your Destiny* (Alachua, FL: Bridge-Logos Publishers, 2001).

and I began to rise up in my spirit.

I found it amazing how God was causing people to give me particular books to read. Prophetic preachers to listen to, and every avenue I was going down, the content was showing me God's provision for inner healing, direction, and enlarging my mind-set, to help me to get out of the "small box" I was in and give me a new vision. God was bringing me out of my two-dimensional "vision" and mind-set, to a three-dimensional vision and mind-set. God was giving me depth of vision. I was beginning to see things that I had never seen before.

If we want new things to happen in our life, it is imperative for us to get out of the old mind-set and habits we have been performing with and in.

I knew God was doing a new thing in me. He was and still is in the process of restoring my soul and altering my thinking.

When you entertain certain thoughts in the privacy of your own mind, you may be tempted to excuse yourself by saying, "what harm can I do?" A lot! Ultimately, you become whatever you meditate on! Solomon said, "For as he thinketh in his heart, so is he" (Proverbs 23:7).

When evil sets out to tear you down, it doesn't start with an act; it starts with a thought. Now thoughts are not yours just because they come into your mind. No, they only become yours when you allow them to move in and rearrange the furniture.

A thought left to ramble through your mind can attach itself to a weakness or an event in your past and feed on it. The stronger it grows, the weaker you become until finally all your strength is drained away. Don't let that happen to you. Paul writes, "take captive every thought to make it obedient to Christ" (2 Corinthians 10:5). In other words, take your thoughts captive before they take you captive.

In Ephesians 4, Paul writes, "put off...the old man... put on the new man..." There are some old clothes you've got to take off when you commit yourself to a God— given goal—like old thinking patterns, old attitudes, and old behaviours. You may not even want to admit that you're still wearing those old clothes, but the truth is you can't put on the new man until you first take off the old one.[23]

I was right at this spot. I find it amazing how God gives you your spiritual food at the right time. God was speaking to me and leading me, and He was doing a new thing in my life.

After Geraldine died, it took me the best part of a year and a quarter to overcome that spirit of offence that was pounding on the door of my heart. Now I knew in my heart that I had totally forgiven people both inside and outside of the church. If I were to leave the church just because of picking up on offence, it would not have been living in victory, but in defeat and I *would have played into Satan's hands.*

However, as soon as I had overcome that attack, God was using the passage from Bob Gass's book and other books preparing the way forward for me. However, most of all God opened up a Scripture from *Isaiah 43:18-19* whereby I made a decision. All of these books and Scriptures were as if God was giving me a road map for my future journey.

The process of moving from my old church assembly was set in motion. It says in *Isaiah 43:18-19, "Do not remember the former things, nor consider the things of old. Behold, I will do a new thing, now it shall spring forth; shall you not know it? I will even make a road in the wilderness and rivers in the desert."*

I knew God was saying it was time to go. I release you. I had been in the same Christian assembly all my Christian life, twenty-seven years. I needed the space to remove the old clothes and put on the new clothes. In addition, my identity was no longer in Mike and Ger anymore, but Mike on his own. The question was, who is Mike or Michael? What does Mike want or not want? It was like

---

23 Ibid.

taking off the old clothes of thinking patterns, old attitudes, and old behaviours. It was imperative for me to leave because if I had stayed, it would have been next to impossible to take off the old clothes. I had to leave to be open to hear and to do the new things God was saying and doing in me.

I heard a preacher say that it is very hard for your old acquaintances to take any label they have on you, off you. I agree fully.

So there I was, in the midst of my old acquaintances, and God was changing my mind-set and desiring to do a new thing in me and through me. My old acquaintances, being very familiar with my thinking pattern, my behaviour and serving pattern for years, had me labelled. This is who he is, and what he does. That is just the way life is. Now that old label had to come off. God is doing a new thing, and the old ways are about to go. Change is hard enough to achieve on its own. It's hard to leave old ways behind in the midst of acquaintances who do not understand, cannot appreciate, or allow one to change as the Lord is directing. It is just that they cannot see the internal work that the Lord is doing in me.

I was willing to take off those old clothes and put on the new ones and keep in pace with what God was directing me to do. Some people might never want to take off the old clothes; they may be too comfortable in them. They may be too insecure to remove the old clothes, or they may be too fearful about how they might look in the new clothes, or too fearful or insecure to be different from the crowd. It might be too challenging and demanding for them. They might not have the courage to take the risk. To do something new is not easy—one takes the risk of being misunderstood. However, it is of paramount importance for me to obey God rather than please man.

John 3:8 says, ***"The wind blows where it wishes, and you hear the sound of it, but cannot tell where it comes from and where it goes. So is everyone who is born of the Spirit,"*** Sometimes the Holy Spirit is described as the wind. He speaks to whom He wishes and when He speaks to you, you hear it but those around you do not understand it because the word was not given to them.

However, when you obey, it is only after some time that the people around you will see the fruit of what you obeyed coming forth. Then they will understand. The Holy Spirit interprets spiritual things to spiritual people and the carnal mind does not understand it. **Romans 8:7** says, **"Because the carnal mind is enmity against God; for it is not subject to the law of God, nor indeed can be."** Therefore, it is no wonder that Jesus said to Nicodemus in verse 7, who was a Pharisee, that you must be born again. That is, to be spiritually awakened by the Holy Spirit.

I had it in the back of my mind for a few years to write this book, but not too long after Geraldine died, I felt the Lord impressing upon my heart a sense that I *must* write this book. This is a very new thing for me to do. I have never been down this road before and at this stage, I have been writing this book for the last two and a half years. I have been putting together all these wonderful real life testimonies of how God has transformed our lives, and how He has led us in a straight path. He has worked wonders in our lives, so that you, the reader, might get to know how precious, wonderful and powerful the Lord is and how much He loves us.

Since the end of December 2009, when the Lord spoke to me from *Isaiah 43:18-19* about leaving behind the old, and His declaration of a *new thing,* these words, *"new thing"* have come to my attention so many times.

I have played the guitar for over forty years, and in February 2010, I put the guitar down and bought a digital piano. I love playing it all the time. That is another "new thing."

Then in November 2010, Pastor Joe Corry, whom I mentioned earlier, spoke prophetically over me.

He said: *"Break through—a 'new thing,' the old things are over, everything from beginning to end. People will marvel at you. They thought you were finished, washed up—amazed and wonder at you— you have changed. Two thousand eleven [2011] will be your year—the start of a great change."*

I was so encouraged that God just confirmed to me through this prophetic message, the Word from *Isaiah 43:18-19* that I had believed and acted upon a year earlier. The Lord was reassuring me that I had heard correctly from Him so that I would not stumble and doubt, by telling myself that I got it wrong when so many people around me thought that I did get it wrong. Furthermore, and this will be encouraging to Pastor Joe Corry, much of what he spoke about prophetically to me has already happened. Many thanks, Joe. Keep on hearing the way you are hearing.

When Pastor Joe went on with his message that day about vision and destiny, I heard challenging words like:

- When you have your hands on something—God cannot take over.
- When you are sick and tired of being sick and tired, you are on the brink of something that God wants to do.
- There is an author named Jack Cranfield, and one of his books is called *"The Success Principles(TM): How to Get from Where You Are to Where You Want to Be"* A comment from it—"Information will be denied to you until you come to your vision."
- A closed mind creates cultures and traditions.
- I cannot resolve a problem with the same mind-set that created it.
- Avoid every thought that weakens you. Read a book that is going to put value into you. Tell yourself you can.
- God sometimes brings you to a place where you have no other choice.
- Progress is impossible if you keep doing the same things you have always done.
- If God is telling you to give something up it means He has something better for you, but you have to give it up and trust Him. Let go of the old. There it is again, letting go of the old.

God has been leading me on a path of new things all the way since then. It is quite amazing and exciting.

I am moving on and I do not quite know where I am going to end up. *Now that is a walk of faith.*

For the past twenty-seven years, I have been working in the trades of carpentry, tiling, and painting. A few months after Geraldine died, I realised that my body got very weak. I was struggling with the labouring work associated with these trades. Even though my body was aching, I tried to struggle on because I had a big bill to pay. I only continued because I was fearful of stopping. Working in these trades were the means I had of earning money. No work meant no income and I had no other alternative put in place, as there were so many other things crowding in on me.

However, during Christmas 2011, I knew I had to look back on the notes of the preaching that Pastor Joe Corry gave in 2010. Within these notes, I knew that God was really speaking to me. My body was screaming at me. Therefore, I woke up and took great note of what God had been reminding me of a year before this. Now I was hearing and ready to obey. The comment that clinched it for me from Pastor Joe's message was: If God is telling you to give something up it means He has something better for you, but you have to give it up and *trust Him*. Let go of the old. When you have your hands on something God cannot take over.

I made up my mind to retire from the old work pattern, and I chose not to worry and trust Jesus for the future.

The next day I took all of my tools out of my estate car and put them back in the shed. As I had to get a new car in February 2012, I said to the Lord that the new car would be a saloon type car [sedan] to stop me returning to the old trades I loved so well. Then two days later, I was reminded that in *1 Kings 19:19-21* in the Old Testament the prophet Elijah called Elisha into ministry. *Verse 21* says, *"So Elisha turned back from him, and took a yoke of oxen and slaughtered them and boiled their flesh, using the oxen's equipment, and gave it to the people, and they ate. Then he arose and followed Elijah, and became his servant."*

That put an excitement in my heart. I had just done something a bit similar. Elisha slaughtered his own oxen and cooked them with the oxen's equipment. In doing so, he was making a statement that he was not going back to the old ways and made sure that there was no avenue back.

The last twenty years have been very frustrating and difficult at times, but I let God do a thorough work in me. Moreover, He is never in a hurry. He had me in a constraining box or cave as was described. For all of those years He was developing patience, peace and character in me, and all for a wonderful purpose that I hope yet to walk into.

Jesus has been transforming me bit by bit over the past twenty-nine years from that shell of restriction I was in, prior to inviting Him into my life. Now I am looking forward to having all those restrictions totally removed and walking into the freedom that the Lord has for me. As long as I have the openness of heart to hear and the willingness to obey Him, I can shed off any baggage that would weigh me down. This will enable me to fly and shine like a butterfly.

Metamorphosis means a change of form; the result of such a change; (Biol.) transformation, as of a chrysalis into a winged insect; (fig.) a complete change of character, purpose, etc. (*The Waverley Modern English Dictionary*).

That is what God the Father does with all people who begin to trust Jesus and live for Him. He takes them out of captivity (that slavery to disobey Him) and begins the process of transforming them into the image of His Son, Jesus Christ, and teaches them how to fly and to be free. He transfigures them.

Somebody told me recently that a person did an experiment with a caterpillar. He tried to quicken the process of the caterpillar transforming into a butterfly by breaking off the shell. The result of that exercise was that the caterpillar did transform into the butterfly but never developed the strength to fly as a butterfly. What a tragedy.

I see something similar with us. When we are going through a trial and it is lasting longer than we desire, we may get tired of waiting on the Lord to bring something to pass or completion. Eventually, we give up, resorting to our old ways of doing something ourselves or of losing patience with it. If we have done that, we have gained nothing and learned nothing, and we fall short of the strength needed for future situations.

Remember, the grace of God is always there to keep us, so draw on His grace. If the trial becomes unbearable, the Lord will make a way of escape for us. Always, the Lord wants to build strength and the character of Christ into us because we do not know what extra strength we may need to face the difficulties ahead of us. So face them head on with Christ, and allow the Lord to complete His work in us, otherwise we might not last. We only develop patience through trials.

A negative past's only positive function is to be that part of your life that you have learned from and overcome. It is your reference point to show the magnitude of what God has done for you so you can give others hope that He will do it for them.[24]

I hope, by the grace of God, I have achieved this for you.

Dear reader, what I have done in writing this book is put a seal on all those life experiences, and leaving all the baggage behind. I am bringing you to the place where I am about to step into the new chapters that the Lord has for me. These are unknown to me at this time but it is a most exciting time of my life. I have grown and matured in God, and all those years of frustration and striving are over. I was spoken to prophetically at the end of 2010. I was told that my latter days are going to be better than my former days, just as with Job in the Old Testament. I embrace that promise and I know it in my spirit.

The Lord has brought me to a new level of trusting Him. I believe I have come to the place the Apostle Paul talks about in *1 Timothy 6:6, "Now godliness with contentment is great gain."* He continues to say in *verse 7, "For we brought nothing into this world, and it is certain we can carry nothing out."*

I am so thankful to the Lord that He kept me in my right mind in the midst of all the turmoil I encountered. The outcome could have had tragic consequences if I had turned against God and everybody around me.

I have an excitement in my spirit about the future. God has

24 Liberty Savard, *Shattering Your Strongholds,* (Alachua, FL: Bridge-Logos Publishers, 1992)

spoken prophetically many things over my life. Some of these things have already happened. In addition, as for the other words spoken, I wait with excited expectation! *2 Chronicles 20:20* says, *"Believe in the Lord your God, and you shall be established; believe His prophets, and you shall prosper."* Therefore, we do not take lightly what God has spoken prophetically. We examine it for its scriptural agreement and the fruit that it bears.

I count it a privilege and an honour to be called by God as an ambassador for Christ by being able to proclaim with boldness the good news of the gospel within the contents of this book, which I have worked out and applied to my life over the last thirty years. This is all because of the undeserved mercies that were poured out for me on Calvary.

Chapter 17

The Race of Faith

I AM writing this 48 years from the time of my first competitive swim race. Then, twenty-nine years ago, I entered another kind of race, I began my spiritual race of faith and by the grace of God will finish on the day when I die.

In reading the Scriptures, I have discovered that the Apostle Paul writes about one's life in Christ as a race, endurance to the end, finishing the race and a prize awaiting you at the end.

For example, in **Hebrews 12:12,** the author writes to us about the race of faith:

Verse 1: "Therefore we also, since we are surrounded by so great a cloud of witnesses, let us lay aside every weight, and the sin which so easily ensnares us, and let us run with endurance the race that is set before us."

Verse 2: "Looking unto Jesus, the author, and the finisher of our faith, who for the joy that was set before him endured the cross, despising the shame, and has set down at the right hand of the throne of God."

The heroes of faith are not spectators watching us from Heaven. Rather their lives are witnesses to us, having successfully overcome. The Christian life is often likened to a race (1 Corinthians 9:24; 2 Timothy 4:7). We are to lay aside anything that hinders our progress, particularly every form of sin.[25]

I see a powerful parallel between my youthful competitive swimming events and the spiritual race of faith. Obeying my coach, the prize at the end, the disciplines needed in my lifestyle to be successful, the starting well, pacing myself during the middle of my race, and the strength to finish well, and not to burn myself

---

25 Notes from Spirit-Filled Life ® Bible.

out before the finish. The same structure accompanies my spiritual race of faith. As above, obeying the instructions from the Father—fight the good fight, keeping the faith, endure hardship as a good soldier of Jesus Christ. Avoid entanglement with the affairs of this life so we can please Him who called us. Finally finish the race we started.

Living as a disciple of Jesus, my focus is looking unto Him, who is the author and finisher of my faith. If I took my eyes off Jesus, I might have found out that I would not finish the race. Look at the Apostle Peter, who got out of the boat after the invitation of Jesus. He walked on the water while his eyes were on Jesus. However, when he took his eyes off Jesus and saw himself doing what he should not be doing, he sank into the water. Gravity pulled him down, but Jesus rescued him. That is a great encouraging lesson we can learn from that passage of Scripture.

It is not always easy to be a follower of Christ because His ways are different from the ways of the world. So pardon the pun—we swim against the tide, as it were. When we know what the prize is, by the power of the Holy Spirit, we can endure the hardships when they come.

I can see now that the Lord prepared me for my spiritual race of faith when I was a teenager, through all the different aspects of the swimming events that I have already spoken. At that time, I had absolutely no idea of what I was being prepared for.

In fact, I see now that my spiritual race of faith mirrors my long distance swimming races that I physically participated in, and that I excelled in when I was a young teenager. I am racing this race of faith for twenty-nine years now. I started out with great gusto and then went into a cruise all these last twenty years or more. I was doing a lot of stuff in my spiritual race as if I was still in a physical race (relying on my strength and in my timing when I should have been yielding to the Lord). My thinking was not quite transformed to God's ways as it ought, but He saw my heart.

In November 1993, a man named Bobby Mearns, prophesied over me in the church assembly. As he saw me sitting in church that particular day, he saw me as a man with great zeal in my heart to see the Lord's power displayed. However, he also saw that I was a man to whom the Lord wanted to impart patience and depth of character. He spoke a word from ***Proverbs 16:32,*** ***"He who is slow to anger is better than the mighty, and he who rules his spirit than he who takes a city."***

I had a lot of physical strength and fitness in those days. I was also impatient and prone to anger. He went on to pray that the Lord would enable me to be restrained and formed. God would hold me in a constraining box like that, where the wood for an arrow is kept to mature and dry out and not warp. When it is taken out of the constraining box and fired from the bow, it will hit the target.

You will have seen the process of how God has dealt with me. Some were very hard lessons but they were worth it, because I see now the transforming work that He has helped me achieve throughout the years. I am not the man I was at the beginning of this spiritual race of faith. He has brought me to a place of patience. The anger and frustrations are gone. My faith has increased. I am more committed to Him than I ever was. However, the Lord did not work independently of me. I still have to cooperate with Him.

I had a lot of physical strength in my early Christian days, which led to impatience when I had to wait, and sometimes wait a long time. However, I made it my ambition to have patience and stay in the box because God, through the prophetic word given to me, told me what He was trying to achieve. Therefore, I cooperated with Him and began the long process of calming down. Through that Word, I saw His love and purpose for me. If He had not told me, I am sure I would have struggled a great deal more for a long time, and may even have given up. I have learned that the only way to gain patience is to go through trials. We know now what we get when we pray for patience!

Zechariah 4:6 states, ***"This is the word of the Lord to Zerubbabel: 'Not by might, nor by power but by my spirit,' says the Lord of hosts."***

The Scriptures speak many times of waiting patiently on the

Lord. God also had to deal with my anger. He was doing a perfect work in me and I was letting Him. ***Philippians 1:6*** states, ***"… being confident of this very thing, that He who has begun a good work in you will complete it until the day of Jesus Christ."***

It was no wonder that God put me in a constraining box. I was like a wild stallion that had to be broken in. God saw the potential within me, but there was a big and long work to be done in me until He could shoot me from the bow.

I know that I have come to the place where God wanted me. I let God do His tremendous work in me because I trusted Him and wanted to be like Jesus.

On October 2011, I received another prophetic message from people who knew nothing of me in the natural sense. Their word over me told me that my time in the box, or the cave as they described it, had come to an end. The job was done and it was time to come out. The following was how they described it to me:

> *I see you hiding in a cave for a very long time, and that during that time your face only came out a few times and went back in. The cave was on a side of a mountain. The cave was set in the side of a dam, and the dam is so full of water and you could see the dam walls bulging with the stuff that was hidden behind it and the dam is you and the potential that is in you can explode into what is out there. The cave is your life that has been for such a long time, you have been held in your cave, and you are desperate to come out of that cave. I [the Lord] want you to reach out of that cave and be that man that God said. It's time for you to come out of that cave and it's time for you to go down that passage to the people who are milling about waiting for the word that you bring to them. It is not the next guy, and the next guy, and the next guy. It's you.*[26]

---

26 International Network of Prophetic Centres. Headquarters: Glasgow Prophetic Centre. Spoken by Malcolm. www.glasgow-prophetic-centre.org.uk

God held me in that cave for a very long time and now He says it is time to come out. The job of character building and peace must now be completed. The imagery of the constraining box and the cave are the same things, just two different ways of saying it. However, the Lord and I were active in the cave. I have a load of activities that declare the works of the Lord, events that were acts of faith. It was Christ working within me and through me, but not for everyone to see at that time.

When these people spoke prophetically over me in October 2011, they did not know what was past, present, or future. Nevertheless, I knew. They had no idea that I was in the midst of writing this book. For me, to have started writing this book is "starting to come out of the cave."

Within the last two years, the Lord has stirred my heart and given me the sense of "I must write this book." I have obeyed Him and it has been the most satisfying, rewarding and hardest task to write these chapters—some of whose contents were emotionally very challenging. Yet, to be able to pour out on paper these works that God has done within me, and through me, and to write about individuals that He had me minister to while in my "cave period" has all been a privilege.

The prophetic word that came to me in October 2011, just confirmed to me that I was doing the right thing and moving in the timing and the purposes of God.

The time has come for me to declare very publicly the works that the Lord has done in and through me. To repeat a part of the prophetic word that came to me in October 2011: "It's time for you to come out of the cave and go down that passage to the people who are milling about waiting for the word that you bring to them." Well, for the moment the contents of this book is what I have to say to you.

My desire and prayer is that as you complete reading the contents of this book, and will have the desire to start this race of faith with Jesus. On the other hand, if you are in the race already, that you will be encouraged to keep going in your race of faith. You may not have a long distance race ahead of you as I have had. You may only have a 50-meter dash as it were, God only knows that. I encourage you to start the race, and more importantly finish it.

In *John 17:1-5,* Jesus is praying for himself:

> *Verse 1: Jesus spoke these words, lifted up His eyes to heaven and said, "Father, the hour has come, glorify your Son, that your Son, also may glorify you."*

> *Verse 2: As you have given Him authority over all flesh to as many as you have given Him.*

> *Verse 3: and this is eternal life that they may know you, the only true God, and Jesus Christ whom you have sent.*

> *Verse 4: I have glorified you on earth, I have finished the work, which you have given Me to do.*

> *Verse 5: And now, O Father, glorify Me together with Yourself, with the glory which I had with You before the world was."*

There was my prize! *Verse 3*: Eternal life is to know God, and Jesus Christ whom the Father has sent.

It is all about relationship.

I read of another person in the Old Testament whom God held in a constraining box or cave-like period. That was Moses. This story is in *Exodus, Chapters 1 and 2.* I saw how God orchestrated events to keep him alive at birth. In addition, how He orchestrated for Moses to grow up in Pharaoh's palace getting a good education while observing all about government and leadership.

He never forgot his roots as a Jew. When he was forty years old, he saw the injustice the Egyptians were imposing on his own fellow Jews. He started to take things into his own hands and killed an Egyptian. He then had to flee out of Pharaoh's sight and ended up in the desert, where he got married and had a job of tending sheep. However, all the time God was shaping him and moulding him, until such time when He saw that Moses was ready. He would now do things God's way, and in His strength and timing.

I dare say, all these events were no accident! God had a plan and a job for Moses to perform some eighty years in life to lead the nation of Israel out of Egypt, which is symbolic of the land of slavery. When I was not a Spirit-filled Christian, I too had my soul in slavery under bondage. But now I was "in Christ" and no longer in captivity, and as I looked at Moses' desert experience, I was encouraged that God had a future purpose for my cave-like experience even though it was difficult at times.

He was giving me a reason for living. He was giving me hope in my heart. ***Romans 5:5*** states, ***"Now hope does not disappoint, because the love of God has been poured out in our hearts by the Holy Spirit who was given to us."***

God was enabling me to have a long-term perspective. God was using all the good and bad experiences I had and was making something good and positive out of them. Nothing is wasted when yielded to Christ. He was purposing to make those negative experiences into positive new experiences. The Lord was using all my past for His kingdom and His glory and His purposes.

From the imagery of Jesus being the potter and I being the clay, it was important for me to be pliable in His hands. First, He had to do a demolition job on my old shape so that He could remould me into the shape that He needed to accomplish His purposes.

The prize, of course, is in knowing Christ and all these setbacks and difficulties were achieving a purpose. They were causing me to draw close to Him, and in doing that, I was getting to know Him more.

The Lord had taught me through my experiences in my sporting career to push through the pain barriers in gaining physical fitness and hence, I was able to achieve what I did. I was applying those same principles to my spiritual race of faith, and by God's grace, I will finish the race.

In any competition, the number of those who start the race is always greater than the number of those who finish. And, of course, the number who win the race is far smaller, only one in fact. Everyone gets a t-shirt; only

one gets the gold medal.

In the spiritual race that is our life, we do not compete with one another. Instead, we push ourselves to better our own previous best. Every year we are to work hard to improve so that in the end we win. To finish well is success. It means that when we cross the finish line, we have a vital and growing spiritual life.

What does the New Testament define as success for a follower of Jesus? When it is all over and we stand alone before Him, what are the standards by which we are judged by the Lord?

As I read the New Testament, I have found three things that Jesus views as crucial to the success of His followers. They are:

1. *Faithfulness.*
2. *Fruitfulness.*
3. *Finishing well.*[27]

---

27 Neil Cole, *Organic Leadership,* (Grand Rapids: Baker Publishing Group, 2009).

Acknowledgments

THE writing of this book has been smouldering in the background of my mind for many years, but since Geraldine died, I got the determination actually to do it. I am grateful to my children for allowing me to mention them as I have done in the book, especially my eldest son, Marc, who I have mentioned in more detail. I want to thank Matthew, Simon, Elena, and Jessica for their patience with me over the past three and a half years while writing, as my mind was very much preoccupied with trying to recall and formulate all my thoughts onto paper.

As the author, and being so close to the subject I was writing, I needed the honesty of good friends for perspective. My four good friends were Honora Meade, Frank and Mary Smyth, and Mary Tighe, who were so encouraging and patient towards me. They had to spend a lot of time listening to me and examining sections of the contents I was writing. They gave me the honest, outside views and comments that were needed, highlighting any blind spots that I had, as I alone did not see everything that needed changing.

I also want to thank Lloyd and Peggy Hildebrand and all the team at Bridge-Logos for their wonderful work and help in getting this book published.

Finally, I want to thank the God of Abraham, Isaac and Jacob whose Son Jesus, the Messiah, has given me a testimony and the testimonies I have shared in this book.

Appendix

God's Plan of Salvation, Received by Faith

A SPIRITUAL law is a truth established by the Word of God, the Bible. This applies to everybody universally. If we disobey any of them, we bear the consequences of our disobedience. On the other hand, if we obey the instructions, we prosper and are kept safe and protected. God fixes the law forever. In **Mark 13:31** Jesus is saying, *"Heaven and earth will pass away, but My words will by no means pass away."* So what He says stays fixed forever.

God has always been motivated by love. When we read the words in the Bible, this theme shines throughout. Let us first go back to the fifth book of Moses and establish this fact: Deuteronomy 7:7-9 "The Lord did not set His love on you nor choose you because you were more in number than any other people, for you were the least of all peoples; but because the Lord loves you, and because He would keep the oath which He swore to your fathers, the Lord has brought you out with a mighty hand, and redeemed you from the house of bondage [slavery], *from the land of Pharaoh king of Egypt. Therefore know that the Lord your God, He is God, the faithful God who keeps covenant and mercy for a thousand generations with those who love Him and keep His commandments." This truth still holds true for today. God loves you and offers a wonderful plan for your life.*[28]

God's unconditional love is shown in **John 3:16,** *"For God so loved the world, that He gave His only begotten Son, that whoever believes in Him should not perish but have everlasting life."* Jesus outlined God's plan when He

28 Bill Bright, Campus Crusade for Christ.

said in *John 10:10, "I have come that they may have life, and that they may have it more abundantly."*

God has always wanted a perfect unbroken relationship with man. Like every family household, there are boundaries and guidelines to live by to maintain peace and order in it. God and man are no exception. *Genesis 2:15-17: "Then the Lord God took the man and put him in the garden to tend and keep it. And the Lord God commanded the man, saying, 'Of every tree of the garden you may freely eat; but of the tree of the knowledge of good and evil you shall not eat, for in the day that you eat of it you shall surely die.'"*

However, the serpent came and planted doubt that led Eve to question the truth of God's Word. Eve was tempted and ate of the forbidden fruit. She then gave the fruit to Adam. He likewise, failed to obey God's command, and ate the forbidden fruit. As soon as they ate that fruit, *"Then the eyes of both of them were opened, and they knew they were naked; and they sewed fig leaves together and made themselves coverings" (Genesis 3:7).* This is the first time Adam and Eve knew good and evil, right and wrong. In *Genesis 3:8,* we see that after they ate the forbidden fruit, they hid themselves from the presence of God. They became fearful.

Before Adam and Eve disobeyed God's command, they lived in innocence. They had total freedom to use of all God allowed. They were unashamed. Father used to come down to them in the cool of the evening and had fellowship with them. In other words, He had a chat with them.

Disobedience broke fellowship with God. In that condition of disobedience, they were put out of the Garden of Eden. God did not want them to eat from the fruit of the tree of life and live forever in a state of sin. *Genesis 3:22-24: "Then the Lord God said, 'Behold, the man has become like one of Us, to know good and evil. And now, lest he put out his hand and take also of the tree of life, and eat, and live forever'— therefore the Lord God sent him out of the garden of Eden to till the ground from which he was taken. So He drove out the man; and He placed cherubim at the east of the garden of Eden and a flaming sword which turned every way, to guard the way to the tree of life."*

Adam and Eve were sinners. They chose to be independent from God. Ever since then, a blockage between God and man entered our hearts. It still plagues us today. Sinfulness (self-will) which is characterised by an attitude of rebellion or passive indifference is what the Bible denotes as sin. Every human spirit is affected by it and every child born into the world inherits it. *Romans 3:23: "For all have sinned, and fall short of the glory of God."* This is the origin of our relationship problem with God. The reason sin is a problem is that God is holy. How can we now relate to our creator God?

In the physical realm, we receive wages for our labour. In the spiritual realm, we also receive wages. *Romans 6:23: "For the wages of sin* [disobedience, rebellion to God] *is death* [spiritual separation from God]*, but the gift of God is eternal life in Christ Jesus our Lord."* Sin robs us of relationship with God now and eternal life in the world to come.

When Adam and Eve ate the fruit of the tree of the knowledge of good and evil, they violated their conscience. We all now know when we do wrong. He has built it into us. Therefore, *"If we say we have no sin, we deceive ourselves, and the truth is not in us" (1 John 1:8).*

There is a gulf between God and man because of our sin. Sin separates man from God. All our best efforts will never reach God's mark and restore the relationship God had with Adam before his disobedience. By our own efforts, we will not live the abundant life Christ promised in *John 10:10* above. God had to provide a way for us to satisfy His requirements, to be reconciled to himself. He sent His only begotten Son Jesus Christ to come to live on Earth. In so doing, Jesus showed us the Father. However, most importantly, the purpose for which Jesus came to earth was to die for us. Look what *2 Corinthians 5:21* says, *"For He* [Father] *made Him* [Jesus] *who knew no sin to be sin for us, that we might become the righteousness of God in Him.* This statement is the positive counterpart to the statement in *verse 19: "That is, that God was in Christ reconciling the world to Himself, not imputing their trespasses to them, and has committed to us the word of reconciliation."*

That God does not impute our trespasses to us. He imputed them instead to Christ, who was sinless in every respect. He bore our sins on the cross and endured the penalty that we deserved that we might become the righteousness of God in Him.[29]

Jesus made a statement to Thomas that nobody on Earth, past, present or future could ever make. Jesus said, *"I am the way, the truth, and the life. No one comes to the Father except through Me" (John 14:6).* Therefore, in order to be right with God the Father, it is imperative to believe His Son Jesus and put our trust in Him.

In *Leviticus,* God showed Moses the method His people were to use to approach Him. He instituted the Levitical priesthood and the sacrificial system. The Levitical priesthood involved daily, weekly and annual sacrifices. All that pointed forward to the ultimate perfect sacrifice. Jesus observed this system while He was on Earth. He knew it was the will of the Father, that He himself be the sacrifice for sin to make peace between man and God. When John the Baptist saw Jesus coming to be baptised, he said. *"Behold! The Lamb of God who takes away the sin of the world!" (John 1:29).* John recognised God's perfect sacrifice.

Hebrews 7:24-28 illustrates what Christ did within a few verses:

But He, because He continues forever, has an unchangeable priesthood. Therefore He is also able to save to the uttermost those who come to God through Him, since He always lives to make intercession for them. For such a High Priest was fitting for us, who is Holy

---

29 Notes from Spirit-Filled Life ® Bible.

harmless, undefiled, separate from sinners, and has become higher than the heavens; who does not need daily, as those high priests, to offer up sacrifices, first for his own sins and then for the people's, for this He did once for all when He offered up himself. For the law appoints as high priests men who have weakness, but the word of the oath, which came after the law, appoints the Son who has been perfected forever.

God did not wait for us to become perfect through our own efforts. He knew we could never attain it. God *"demonstrates His own love towards us, in that while we were still sinners, Christ died for us" (Romans 5:8).* This is the good news.

In *John 3:16* we read, *"For God so loved the world that He gave His only begotten Son, that whoever believes in Him shall not perish but have everlasting life."*

Jesus died on the feast of Passover. He was buried in a new tomb on the evening of Passover before the start of the high Sabbath, which began the Feast of Unleavened Bread. Jesus spent three nights and three days in the grave. He rose from the dead on the Feast of First Fruits. His resurrection proved that His death satisfied God the Father's requirement for sin. It also fulfilled the prophecies in Moses and the Prophets concerning the Messiah to come. His Resurrection confirmed Jesus is the promised Messiah. Jesus our Lord and Saviour was Jewish. He kept the feasts of the Lord.[30] By understanding the prophetic nature of these feasts; we come to see a bigger picture of the life and ministry of Christ. We also begin to see that He has more to do. He is coming again to rule and reign as He promised. Paul wrote in *1 Corinthians 15:3-8,* *"For I delivered to you first of all that which I also received: that Christ died for our sins according to the Scriptures, and that He was buried, and that He rose again the third day according to the Scriptures, and that He was seen by Cephas, and then by the*

---

30 Leviticus 23.

twelve. After that He was seen by over five hundred brethren at once, of whom the greater part remain to the present, but some have fallen asleep. After that He was seen by James, then by all the apostles. Then last of all He was seen by me also, as by one born out of due time."

Let me recap quickly on what has been said so far as it applies to me:

1. God loves me and wants me to be in right relationship with Him.
2. I am sinful and separated by sin from God. This prevents me from knowing and experiencing God's plan for my life.
3. Jesus Christ is God's only acceptable provision for my sin. Through Christ, I can come to know and experience God's love and plans for my life.
4. What must I do now to apply this good news to my life?

The answer is: I must acknowledge my sin problem. I must admit that my ways of dealing or trying to cope with it are inadequate. I must accept that God has a better solution to my sin problem. As God continues to draw me and persuade me that Jesus is His answer, I need to agree with Him, surrender to Him as an admirer, invite Jesus into my heart, and receive Him as my Saviour and Lord.

The word "believed" is first mentioned in the Bible in *Genesis 15:6* where it talks about Abraham, *"And he* [Abraham] *believed in the Lord, and He* [God the Father] *accounted it to him for righteousness."*

The word "believe" is an action word. It means that when God speaks to us as He did to Abraham; we hear it and put it into action. When Abraham did what God told him to do, it was accounted to him for righteousness. The same principle applies to us when we do His commands. Believing and doing are inseparable. We do what we believe. We read the Scripture in *2 Corinthians 5:21, "For He made Him who knew no sin to be sin for us, that we might become the righteousness of God in Him."* The reality of

170

this Scripture is that when we receive Christ and accept what He has done for us on the Cross, it makes us righteous before the Father. *"But as many as received Him* [Christ], *to them He gave the right to become children of God, even to those who believe in His name" (John 1:12).*

To receive Christ, you have to receive Him by faith. If we have something in our physical possession, we do not need faith because we have it already. Faith is described to us in *Hebrews 11:1, "Now faith is the substance of things hoped for, the evidence of things not seen."* To phrase it another way, "Faith actualises what it realises in the unseen realm."

Whenever we read the Scriptures, we read with faith in our hearts. We accept them to be true for us even though we see them not with our naked eye, and in due course, as long as we do not resort to unbelief, those promises will become real to us in its time. *Hebrews 11:6* exhorts us a bit further when it says, *"But without faith it is impossible to please Him, for he who comes to God must believe that He is, and that He is a rewarder of those who diligently seek Him."*

Prayer to Receive Christ by Faith and Personal Invitation

Dear Lord Jesus, I believe you are the Son of God. You died on the Cross for my sins. You rose from the dead that I might have eternal life. I need you. I now open the door of my heart to receive you as my Saviour and Lord. I confess I am a sinner before you. Forgive me of my sins, my independent living, and come into my heart. I come off the throne of my life and place you on it. Let your will be done in me as it is in Heaven. Shape me and mould me to be like you. Change my life, Lord, and give me the power to live for you through the Holy Spirit. Amen.

The Bible says, *"If we confess our sins, He is faithful and just to forgive us our sins, and to cleanse us from all unrighteousness" (1 John 1:9).*

Romans 10:9-10 says: *"That if you confess with your mouth the Lord Jesus and believe in your heart that God has raised Him from the dead, you will be saved. For with the heart one believes unto righteousness, and with the mouth confession is made unto salvation,"*

When I said this prayer from my heart, Jesus came into my life as He had promised. He filled my heart with such love, excitement, and peace that I had to tell somebody about what I had just done. It will be the same for you too, dear reader. If you have just now asked Jesus into your heart, then tell someone. Confess it. You have just become a child of God. A miracle has just happened in your life. A child of God is a disciple. A disciple is an imitator and follower of the Lord.

In Ephesians 2:4-10, it is written:

But God, who is rich in mercy, because of His great love with which He loved us, even when we were dead in trespasses, made us alive together with Christ (by grace you have been saved), and raised us up together, and made us sit together in the heavenly places in Christ Jesus, that in the ages to come He might show the exceeding riches of His grace in His kindness towards us in Christ Jesus. For by grace you have been saved through faith, and that not of yourselves; it is the gift of God, not of works, lest anyone should boast. For we are His workmanship, created in Christ Jesus for good works, which God prepared beforehand that we should walk in them.

This following passage summarises the change that takes place in our life after we ask Jesus to be our Lord and Saviour. When we humble ourselves and surrender our will, to invite Jesus to be Lord of our life, great things happen!

1. He comes into our heart and will. *Revelation 3:20, "Behold, I stand at the door and knock. If anyone hears My voice and opens the door, I will come into him and dine with him, and he with Me."*

2. His Holy Spirit confirms to our hearts that we have eternal life. The Apostle John put it this way. *"And this*

is the testimony: that God has given us eternal life, and this life is in His Son. He who has the Son has life; he who does not have the Son of God does not have life. These things I have written to you who believe in the name of the Son of God, that you may know that you have eternal life, and that you may continue to believe in the name of the Son of God" (1 John 5:11-13).

3. The huge burden of guilt and sin is lifted. It is great to realise that going to Heaven when we die is a present. *"It is the gift of God" (Ephesians 2:8).* This means we do not have to live our lives in fear of death in case we did not get enough good things done to please God to get us into Heaven. What a relief to know God will let me into Heaven because I accepted His gift by believing Jesus' death on Calvary paid for my sin. Making Jesus my Lord is seen in how I now live. I have peace in my heart.

4. Our motivation is now driven by the desire to please God. Faithfulness to God now becomes the evidence of our faith. God the Father is looking for imitators who will do God things God's way. Because sin has been the barrier between God and me, God had to *"create in me a clean heart" (Psalm 51:10)* and give me the heart He promised in *Jeremiah 31:33* where He said, *"I will put My law in their minds, and write it on their hearts; and I will be their God, and they shall be My people."* In all of this, God gets the glory.

5. The impact this has on the daily life of a disciple is to make life simple.

Ordinary people have a different motivation now for doing good deeds than we had before we became disciples. We no longer do good to try to earn acceptance with God. *"We are His workmanship, created in Christ Jesus for good works, which God prepared beforehand that we should walk in them" (Ephesians 2:10).* This means that after we become followers of Christ, God has jobs for us that will bring Him glory. Now when we do any good deed for another we cannot take the credit. We must acknowledge that the credit belongs to God who created the job for me in the first place! This stops us from being proud of ourselves.

"For with the heart one believes unto righteousness, and with

the mouth confession is made unto salvation" (Romans 10:10). Our hearts need to be circumcised. What I mean by that is that the hardness of heart that unbelief brings must be removed. If we just agree with our intellect the truth about Jesus Christ and His death on the Cross, it will not result in us doing anything about it. Neither should we rely on our emotions to dictate to us. We receive Jesus Christ by faith as an act of our will. We should not love anyone solely on our emotions; it ought to be an act of our will primarily. That way our actions will be consistent with our newly professed belief.

"There is no fear in love; but perfect love casts out fear, because fear involves torment. But he who fears has not been made perfect in love. We love Him because He first loved us"(1 John 4:18-19).

Jesus is now in Heaven at the Father's right hand. He is a perfect intercessor for all who believe in Him. (See **Hebrews 7:25.**) Another thing Jesus does for us is that He takes away our fear of death. **Hebrews 2:14-15: *"Inasmuch then as the children have partaken of flesh and blood, He Himself likewise shared in the same, that through death He might destroy him who had the power of death, that is, the devil, and release those who through fear of death were all their lifetime subject to bondage."***

Jesus informs us in **John 10:10, *"The thief does not come except to steal, and to kill, and to destroy. I have come that they may have life, and that they may have it more abundantly."*** The aim of Jesus Christ for all mankind is to set them free. All through the centuries, God is the one who initiated love towards us. He longs for our response to love Him in return. We show our love to Him by doing what He says. However, as the Scripture in *1 John 4:18-19* just mentioned, we need to see His love for ourselves before we have any chance of responding to Him with our love.

Jesus came to transfigure and to transform the lives of men and women. Jesus gives a new glory to everything He touches. He turns the useless into the useful. He turns the dull, colourless into the sparkling, and vital. He takes any wasted life and transforms it. He takes a blundering fisherman named Peter, a man of impulse and unstable as water and makes him into a rocklike stable character. He takes a thunderbolt fiery—tempered man named John, capable of calling down fire from Heaven on certain misguided villagers who refuse a night's lodging and changes him into the Apostle of love. He takes a greedy, grasping tax collector named Matthew and sets him to writing a timeless gospel. He takes a demon–possessed woman named Mary and makes her the first herald of His Resurrection. He takes Saul of Tarsus the greatest menace of the Christian Church and turns him into the greatest missionary of the Church. And He is the same Christ still. He still changes every human life that is willing to surrender itself to Him. He still accepts every gift we put in His hands—not to cheapen and spoil but to transform and glorify. He is here to change us for the better.[31]

Moving Forward to Growing Spiritually

It is important that you move forward from here. Asking Jesus into your heart is the start. The next step is to cultivate this new right relationship with God. A good model to use is based on what Jesus taught in the "Lord's Prayer."

In a quiet place, draw near to the Father every day, talk to Him. Break down in small sections the "Lord's Prayer." This prayer is not a formula for repetition. It is an outline for expansion.

First, *"Our Father in heaven, hallowed be your Name."* Praise Father, give Him thanks for who He is and what He calls himself.

Second, *"Thy Kingdom come ..."* Pray His rule, authority and His peace to come, bit by bit into every area of your life.

Third, *"your will be done on earth as it is in heaven ..."* Be willing to forsake your will being done for His will to be done in your life. Take time to examine the condition of your own heart and will before a holy God who is your King. This may take some

---

31 Harold G. Norris.

time to get a grip of, as you will need to get started in reading the Bible to get to know His will and His heart. Do not be anxious about this, He will guide you.

Fourth, *"Give us this day our daily bread …"* Matthew 4:4 says, *"Man does not live by bread alone, but by every Word that comes from the mouth of God."* Start to be spiritually nourished with the Word of God. Start by reading the milk of God's Word—the Gospel of John, for example. Get to know about our Saviour, Jesus Christ. Tell the Lord every other need you have. Build a close relationship with Him.

Fifth, *"and forgive us our sins as we also forgive everyone who is indebted to us …"* Take time to forgive others who have wronged you in any way. If you are being convicted (or convinced) of having wronged another, part of the growing process is to go to the other and ask their forgiveness. Learn to get free from unforgiveness by forgiving those who have wronged you. Unforgiveness will only damage you. We will only be forgiven our trespasses by God as we forgive others their trespasses. I encourage you a bit further, to those who curse you, let your soul be silent; and let your soul be like dust to everyone.

Sixth, *"and do not lead us into temptation, but deliver us from the evil one …"* Ask the Lord to steer you clear of danger and temptation, but you must be careful about your own weak areas in your own lives. Do not go to the place that will cause you to fall. You need to be wise, also ask God to strengthen you. Ask the Lord to show you an alternative that will keep you safe.

Start to be spiritually nourished and read the gospels. They will show you about Jesus and the early disciples. If you find that He is telling you about something you need to obey, make sure you do it, you will discover it will be of great benefit. Read the Scriptures as though you are reading a love letter, because in fact that is exactly what it is to you. Ask the Lord to empower you by His Holy Spirit every day as you go and live life. You are living now as a spiritual person relying on the Lord. Begin to live in the abundance that the Lord has for you. Be blessed in your journey.

APPENDIX

Should you need more information you can contact me.

Website: www.fromadversitytofreedom.com

Email: jesustransformsus@gmail.com